BUILT TO SERVE

BUILT TO SERVE

The Surprisingly Simple Path
to Unstoppable Advisory Success

PAUL L. DURSO

BUILT TO SERVE
The Surprisingly Simple Path to Unstoppable Advisory Success

FIRST EDITION

ISBN   978-1-5445-5096-1   *Hardcover*
       978-1-5445-5095-4   *Paperback*
       978-1-5445-5097-8   *Ebook*

To every advisor who's ever said, "There has to be a better way to grow my practice"…and then went back to refreshing their online leads dashboard anyway—this book is for you.

To the spreadsheet wizards, the late-night planners, the skeptics-turned-co-planners, and the advisors still stuck on marketing autopilot—I see you. You're not lazy. You're just trapped in a system that taught you to chase instead of serve.

This book is dedicated to the ones bold enough to stop chasing and start building something real.

To the advisors who've stepped off the seminar circuit and into the living rooms of their clients' lives—thank you. Your courage to serve, teach, and plan alongside your clients is what's transforming this profession from a hustle into a calling.

To every client who said, "I finally understand my plan!"—thank you. You're why this book exists.

May this be the moment you stop prospecting and start growing—by being Built to Serve.

CONTENTS

To every advisor who has shaped this book—whether you're the spreadsheet zealot who color-codes everything, the social media magician chasing the next big #instalead, the "I'll-get-around-to-it" specialist who hasn't opened their inbox in a week, or the fearless visionary dreaming up tomorrow's breakthroughs—thank you. You've shown me how hilariously diverse (and sometimes maddening) our industry can be.

To the One above all, God, for sparking the ideas and humor woven throughout these pages—and for reminding me that true wisdom is best approached with humility and gratitude. You've been my ultimate compass.

So here's to you all: the meticulous, the lazy-yet-charming, the creative, the borderline bonkers, and everyone in between. May your compliance checks go smoothly, your client referrals overflow, and your coffee cup always be full. You've made this journey worth writing about. And on a serious note—thank you for inspiring me to share what I've learned, one misadventure at a time.

VICTORY HILL

Sustainable Growth Requires Long-Term Thinking

When I was in eighth grade, I had an opportunity that seemed destined to change my young life—or at least impress a certain girl I wanted to date.

Our youth group organized a weekend trip to Whispering Pines Ranch, a sprawling estate nestled among rolling hills and dense woodlands. The ranch was renowned for its majestic horses. For a city kid like me, it promised adventure and, perhaps more importantly, a chance to catch the eye of Sandy, the girl who had been occupying my thoughts for months.

As we gathered in the main corral, the ranch leader stepped forward. "Who here has ridden a horse before?" he asked. Hands shot up, including mine. "Keep your hand up if you've ridden ten times or more." Some hands went down. "Twenty times?" More hands lowered. "A hundred times?" he challenged. Only one hand remained high and proud—mine.

I felt a surge of pride as I puffed out my chest. This was my moment to shine in front of Sandy. The truth, however, was I'd never so much as sat on a pony ride at a fair. But why let the truth get in the way of a good story—or in this moment, the chance to impress Sandy?

The ranch hands began assigning horses to each rider. While most of my peers were matched with gentle mares and seasoned trail horses, I was led to a stall that seemed almost otherworldly. Inside stood Thunderbolt, a horse whose very presence commanded respect. The ranch leader looked at me with a mix of admiration and caution. "Thunderbolt here has raced in the Preakness and the Belmont Stakes. He's powerful and spirited—a true champion. We don't usually let anyone ride him, but with your experience, you should be just fine."

My heart pounded. The reality of my little white lie hit me like a freight train. As I mounted Thunderbolt for the first time, I was acutely aware of every taut muscle beneath me. He was colossal, a bundle of raw energy waiting to explode. I had no idea how to hold the reins properly, let alone control a racehorse eager to run.

We set off on the trail, and I was positioned at the back with Lisa, our youth leader's wife, while Sandy rode somewhere up front. Every so often, I'd catch a glimpse of her laughter floating back on the wind, and I'd fervently wish for a chance to ride beside her. But each time I tried to nudge Thunderbolt forward, the ranch hands would gently but firmly guide me back. "Stay behind," they cautioned. "Thunderbolt isn't used to the trail. He might bolt if he's up front."

After a leisurely ride and a picnic lunch where I managed a brief, awkward conversation with Sandy—still pretending to be a seasoned rider—I remounted Thunderbolt for the return journey. The ranch leader gathered us one final time.

"Up ahead is Victory Hill," he announced. "When we clear the woods, the horses will start to run. Let them. They'll race up the hill and head straight back to the stables. It's a thrill, but hold on tight!"

A mix of excitement and dread washed over me. We entered the narrow trail, the canopy of trees giving way to the open sky. Suddenly, the horses ahead surged forward. Thunderbolt tensed beneath me, muscles coiling like springs. Before I could brace myself, he launched into a full gallop.

The world blurred. Trees and fellow riders whipped past as Thunderbolt unleashed his full speed. I was no longer a rider but a passenger clinging desperately to a runaway. Panic set in as I bounced uncontrollably in the saddle, knuckles white from gripping the reins. Thunderbolt veered close to Lisa's horse. In the chaos, his powerful stride clipped her ankle. She cried out in pain, but there was no stopping now.

One by one, we overtook other horses. Thunderbolt was relentless, his competitive spirit driving us ever faster. By the time we reached the crest of Victory Hill, we were at the front of the pack. Ahead lay the ranch, and I could only hope Thunderbolt would slow down on his own.

We arrived at the stables long before the others. I dismounted shakily, legs like jelly, heart pounding in my ears. As the rest of the group trickled in, I avoided their glances, especially Sandy's. My grand attempt to impress her ended in disaster. Lisa broke her ankle because I couldn't control Thunderbolt. No one cheered for me for being the first one back. Rather, they laughed at me because I looked like a crazy man hanging on for dear life as Thunderbolt charged up Victory Hill. Most importantly, I ripped my shorts somewhere along the way, and as fate would have it, I showed off more than my ego that afternoon.

Did I get the girl? No. Sandy rode off into the sunset with another cowboy. That's okay. My beautiful bride was waiting for me down the road, and we've been riding together ever since. I learned a valuable lesson that day—one that I'd like to share with you.

* * *

As financial advisors, we often find ourselves in a position like my youthful escapade with Thunderbolt. Eager to impress clients and outperform competitors, we seek the fastest horses—the hottest stocks and the trendiest investments—without truly understanding how to handle them. Some of us might boast about our experience, puff out our chests, and position ourselves as seasoned experts. But when it comes time to navigate the unpredictable terrain of the financial markets, many of us hold on for dear life, hoping not to be thrown off.

Just as I had no business riding a racehorse like Thunderbolt without any riding experience, too many advisors get set up for failure by trying to shortcut the learning process. These advisors focus on the endgame—winning the race—without putting in the necessary groundwork. They don't take time to learn how to nurture a portfolio, understand the nuances of market behavior, or build a solid financial "barn" that can weather any storm.

I'm not handing you a pretrained racehorse or a prepackaged success formula with this book. Instead, I want to help you build your stable, raise your horses, and chart your course. I want the pages that follow to help you understand that the ride is smoother—and more rewarding—when you create the groundwork yourself.

The purpose behind this book is to help advisors who love to chase shiny things. The ones who can't get enough of the next big marketing trend in hopes of growing their practice. This book is to help motivate you to *stop chasing prospects* and *start focusing on existing clients*.

Are you this type of advisor? If you are, hear me out. When you switch gears and focus on your current clients, you will grow your business faster, more consistently, and more resiliently than you would via any shiny marketing trend.

As the title suggests, if you want to grow your practice, then you have to stop prospecting. The goal is simple: to guide you through the process of building your stable—from the ground up—with a model that's all about co-planning with your clients.

Together, we'll explore creating a strong foundation, using the right tools when it's time, selecting promising investments (your goals, if you will), and cultivating them into becoming champions.

We'll also talk about something that's not as boring as it sounds and way more effective than 99 percent of financial advisors realize: how co-planning is a service model that leads to success.

The big message: now is the time to stop running the endless race of acquisition and nurture the stables you're in the process of building. By focusing on your foundational elements, you'll achieve success in individual races and also establish a reputation that attracts clients and peers. You'll become the advisor and trainer others look to for guidance, the one who doesn't just ride fast horses but knows how to raise them.

Let's embark on this journey together, ensuring when you choose to ride, you're not just holding on but confidently leading the charge.

Part 1

YOUR FREEDOM'S AT STAKE

CHAPTER 1

THE FREEDOM FRAMEWORK

Building Your Life, Not Just a Financial Practice

The weight of the watch felt heavier than its actual ounces. As I fastened the band around my wrist, the word "BOSS" gleamed up at me, not just as a brand but as a declaration. It was a quiet Tuesday afternoon in Michigan, and I had just done something terrifying and exhilarating: I quit my job.

* * *

I remember that day vividly. I'd just resigned from a firm where I'd been a minor partner—a place that had offered me financial stability but at the cost of something far more valuable: my freedom. I didn't tell anyone about my plan, not even my wife. Instead, I grabbed my father-in-law, Ray, and drove to a department store.

"Why are we here?" Ray asked, puzzled, as we stood at the men's jewelry counter.

"I need to get something," I replied, pointing to a Hugo Boss watch under the glass.

As the salesperson handed it to me, Ray squinted at the dial. "BOSS," he read aloud. "Oh, I get it. You're the boss now."

I smiled. "Close," I said. "I'm the boss of my time."

That watch wasn't just an accessory; it was a symbol of reclaiming control over my life. No longer would someone else dictate my schedule, telling me when to show up or how late to stay. I took back my time, and with it, my life.

In that moment, I realized freedom went beyond a paycheck—it meant regaining autonomy over several aspects of my life. And this realization sparked what I call the Freedom Framework, a set of guiding principles to create stability and genuine independence.

THE FREEDOM OF INCOME

Let's rewind a bit. Before I could even think about being the boss of my time, I had to secure the freedom of income. You see, real success for a financial advisor—or anyone, really—starts with financial stability. Not extravagance, but enough to meet your needs and then some—a "needs-plus" lifestyle.

When I first moved my practice to Charlotte, North Carolina, I made a calculated decision. I was willing to sacrifice immediate income to gain control over my time. I thought time was the most valuable asset, and while that's partly true, I quickly realized you can't have freedom of time without first achieving freedom of income.

Back then, my wife and I sat down to crunch the numbers. How much did we need to maintain our household, support our kids' education, and enjoy modest vacations? We weren't aiming for opulence. Our kids didn't need to attend elite private schools or fly first class. We wanted comfort, not excess.

Understanding this "enough" number was crucial. It wasn't about limiting our aspirations but about defining success on our terms. This clarity allowed me to set realistic income goals, freeing me from the constant chase of more, more, more.

THE FREEDOM OF TIME

With our financial foundation laid down, I didn't have to sacrifice my income to earn this freedom anymore. After all, this freedom is the one resource you can't earn back. Owning my schedule meant being present for my family in ways I hadn't been before. No more missing soccer games because of late appointments or skipping family dinners due to work commitments.

Inspired by Gary Keller's book *The One Thing*, my wife and I adopted a new approach to planning.[1] At the beginning of each year, we sat down with a calendar and plotted our vacations and mission trips—often totaling three months annually. We scheduled our personal time first and planned work around it, not the other way around.

This wasn't just liberating for us; it set a precedent for how I ran my practice. I attracted clients who respected my time because I respected theirs. It created a culture where time was valued, not squandered.

THE FREEDOM OF CHOICE

Achieving freedom of income and time led me to an even more empowering place: the freedom of choice. This is the ability to choose whom you work with and, just as importantly, whom you don't.

I'll never forget the first time I turned away a client. He was a patent attorney who attended one of my seminars. With $10 million

---

1   Gary Keller and Jay Papasan, *The One Thing: The Surprisingly Simple Truth About Extraordinary Results* (Bard Press, 2013).

in assets, he was a dream client on paper. But from our first meeting, red flags popped up. He was meticulous to the point of being overbearing, arriving with a thick binder of documents and an air of self-importance.

After our third meeting, I woke up in a cold sweat. My gut told me this man would make my professional life miserable. Despite the substantial financial gain, I realized no amount of money was worth sacrificing my peace of mind.

I spoke with my then boss and explained my concerns. Together, we crafted a polite but firm letter declining to take him on as a client. As I sent it off, a wave of relief washed over me. I had chosen sanity over income, and it felt incredible.

This freedom of choice wasn't just about avoiding difficult clients. It was about intentionally surrounding myself with people who enriched my life. I joined a group called C12, a gathering of Christian business owners who meet monthly to discuss not just business strategies but also personal growth and community impact.

These monthly meetings became a wellspring of inspiration and support. Surrounded by like-minded individuals, I discovered my business didn't just grow—it flourished in ways I hadn't imagined. The freedom to choose my associations amplified my personal and professional life.

THE FREEDOM OF PURPOSE

There was still a deeper level to reach—the freedom of purpose. This was the most challenging and the most rewarding freedom to attain. It required introspection, courage, and, frankly, a bit of wrestling with my calling.

I didn't start out wanting to be a financial advisor. Far from it. In college, I majored in pastoral studies and psychology at Liberty University, fully intending to become a youth pastor. Helping others was my calling, and I envisioned doing so from the pulpit, not in seminars, client events, or prospect meetings.

When I became a financial advisor, it felt like a detour at best, a derailment at worst. I was frustrated, even angry. Why was I here, crunching numbers when my heart longed for ministry?

The turning point came during a conversation with a close friend, one of a group of guys from Liberty University who was very close to me. During a phone call years ago, I poured my heart out in frustration regarding my vocation.

He said, "You don't need a church's name on your paycheck to be in ministry."

That hit me like a revelation. I realized I could integrate my faith and desire to help others within my financial practice. Years later, this epiphany led me to start a foundation called One Hero, focused on sustainable ministry efforts. Now I dedicate months each year to this cause, seamlessly blending my professional skills with my personal mission.

Achieving the freedom of purpose wasn't a quick journey. It takes years of building the other freedoms—income, time, and choice—to create the space needed for this deeper fulfillment. But once I aligned my work with my core values, everything changed. My practice became more than a business; it became a platform for meaningful impact.

* * *

I glanced at my watch—its face reflecting the soft glow of the setting sun—as I sat on the porch, contemplating the twists and turns my life had taken. Just when you think you've got it all figured out, life has a way of throwing you a curveball.

EMBRACING YOUR JOURNEY

Freedom, I've learned, is not a destination but a journey—a fluid state that ebbs and flows with the tides of life. Just as you can earn these freedoms through hard work and deliberate choices, you can also lose them, sometimes through no fault of your own, and other times because of missteps along the way.

What does all this mean for you? Maybe you're a rookie advisor just getting started, hustling to build your client base. Perhaps you're seasoned but feeling trapped by your schedule or client demands. Wherever you are, consider these four freedoms a roadmap and a mirror.

Ask yourself:

- **Freedom of Income:** What is your "enough"? Are you chasing someone else's definition of success, or have you defined your own?
- **Freedom of Time:** Does your schedule reflect your priorities? Are you investing time in what truly matters to you?
- **Freedom of Choice:** Are you surrounding yourself with people who uplift and inspire you? Do you have the courage to walk away from relationships that drain you?
- **Freedom of Purpose:** What gets you out of bed in the morning? Does your work align with your core values and passions?

The freedoms above are interconnected and subjective. They require self-awareness and deliberate action to achieve and maintain. But the pursuit is worth it. Not just for the milestones you'll reach, but for the person you'll become along the way.

SACRIFICE VERSUS EARNING FREEDOM

There's a fundamental difference between sacrificing to gain a freedom and downright earning a freedom. Sacrifice often implies giving up something valuable in exchange for something else. It's a trade-off. Sometimes it's a necessary step. But earning freedom means you've built a sustainable foundation that supports that freedom without compromising other aspects of your life.

When I left my stable position at a firm in Michigan, I sacrificed immediate income to gain control over my time. It was a calculated risk. I tightened our family's budget, cutting out nonessentials and reassessing our financial priorities. Those early days were not extravagant, and there were definitely moments of struggle. But the sacrifice was a stepping stone, not the end goal.

Earning the freedom of income came later, as a result of building a practice that aligned with my values and served my clients well. It wasn't about a quick win; it was about establishing a sustainable model that provided financial stability without demanding constant sacrifice.

However, sacrifices aren't always voluntary. Sometimes life demands them unexpectedly.

THE UNPREDICTABLE SHIFTS

Take my colleague Kevin, for instance. One ordinary day, his life was upended when his wife was involved in a severe car accident. In a split second, everything changed. Kevin sacrificed not by choice but by necessity. His freedom of time and income took a hit as he devoted himself to her recovery, attending therapy sessions and managing medical bills.

"I thought I had everything under control," he told me one night on the phone. "But life had other plans."

Kevin's experience was a stark reminder that our freedoms are vulnerable to forces beyond our control. He hadn't done anything wrong; he was blindsided by circumstances no one could have predicted.

On the other hand, there are times when we lose freedoms due to our actions—or inactions.

LOSING FREEDOM THROUGH MISSTEPS

Early in my career, after achieving a level of financial success, I became complacent. I said yes to every client and opportunity, ignoring the red flags I had once heeded. The allure of more meetings, more income, and ultimately more success clouded my judgment.

Before long, my schedule was overflowing. I was working late nights, missing family events, and feeling the weight of stress like a heavy backpack I couldn't take off when I wanted to and didn't need to when I had the time. I had inadvertently sacrificed my freedom of time and choice—the very freedoms I had worked so hard to earn.

One evening, I came home and saw my son sitting on the edge of his bed, waiting for me.

"Dad, you missed my soccer game," he said, his eyes reflecting disappointment and a hint of excitement, not because I wasn't there, but because he couldn't wait to tell me he scored two goals.

My heart sank. In my pursuit of more, I had lost sight of what truly mattered. It was a wake-up call. I realized that by overextending myself, I wasn't just losing time; I was eroding the very foundation of my freedoms.

Here was the bigger problem: I wasn't in a position to control my time, so my wife and I had to make some decisions. The easiest decision was to recommit to the principles that had guided me initially. The toughest one was resigning, leaving the only state my kids had ever known, and starting fresh. To be honest, that was one of the toughest decisions of my life. I stood up for what I believed was necessary to regain the balance I had lost.

THE NECESSITY OF VIGILANCE AND ADAPTABILITY

These experiences taught me that maintaining our freedoms requires constant vigilance and adaptability. Life is dynamic, not static. Our circumstances, relationships, and environments are continually changing, and we must be willing to adjust course when needed.

After Kevin's wife began to recover, he found himself at a crossroads. The experience had reshaped his priorities. He decided to restructure his practice to allow for more family time, even if it meant earning less. But this time, it wasn't a sacrifice; it was a choice aligned with his newly defined purpose.

"I realized that freedom isn't just about what you have," he said. "It's about who you become through the trials."

Similarly, unforeseen events like market downturns, health issues, or even global crises can impact our freedoms. The pandemic of 2020, for example, forced many of us to adapt rapidly. Virtual meetings replaced in-person consultations, and the way we manage time and client relationships shifted dramatically.

EMBRACING THE IMPERMANENCE

Understanding the fluid nature of freedom helps us appreciate and nurture it. We must recognize that freedoms can be fragile, requiring care and attention. They are not trophies to be won and placed on a shelf; they're living parts of our lives that need ongoing cultivation.

This impermanence isn't meant to instill fear but to inspire action. It's a call to:

- **Regularly Reassess Your Priorities:** Check in with yourself and your loved ones. Are your actions aligning with your values and goals?
- **Stay Adaptable:** Be willing to pivot when life throws you a curveball. Adaptability is a strength, not a concession.
- **Practice Gratitude:** Appreciate the freedoms you have today. Gratitude enhances your awareness and helps you navigate challenges with a positive mindset.
- **Invest in Resilience:** Build a support system, both personally and professionally, that can help you weather storms when they arise.

THE POWER OF CHOICE IN ADVERSITY

Even when freedoms are lost or compromised, we get to choose how we respond. We can choose to see setbacks as failures or as opportunities for growth. We can let unforeseen circumstances defeat us, or we can let them refine us.

When faced with health issues that forced me to slow down, I initially saw it as a setback. But in that quiet space, I found new perspectives. I deepened my relationships, explored interests I'd neglected, and ultimately emerged with a renewed sense of purpose.

* * *

As the last rays of sunlight dipped below the horizon, I stood up from the porch. The watch on my wrist reminded me not just of being the boss of my time but of the ever-changing journey of freedom. It's a journey filled with peaks and valleys, victories and lessons. Through it all, it's the pursuit and preservation of these freedoms that make the journey worthwhile.

MOVING FORWARD WITH AWARENESS

As you navigate your path, remember that freedom is a gift and a responsibility. It's something to be earned, cherished, and protected. Be mindful of the sacrifices you make. Ensure they're stepping stones rather than permanent trade-offs that deplete other areas of your life.

Accept that life will bring unforeseen changes. You may lose your freedom temporarily or have to fight harder to maintain it. That's okay. What matters is your commitment to reclaiming and nurturing these freedoms whenever possible.

It's not about achieving a perfect state where all freedoms are permanently secured. It's about embracing the fluidity of life, making conscious choices, and continually aligning your actions with your deepest values and purposes.

By doing so, you enrich your life and also inspire those around you to pursue their freedoms with courage and conviction.

Today, when I look down at the watch on my wrist—a bit scuffed now but still ticking faithfully—I'm reminded of that pivotal moment when I chose to take control of my life. Being the "boss" isn't about power or prestige. It's about the freedom to live life on your own terms, guided by purpose and passion.

I invite you to embark on your journey toward these freedoms. Define them for yourself, pursue them relentlessly, and watch how they transform not just your business, but your entire life.

CHAPTER 2

THE FOUR PILLARS OF CHANGE

*Shift from Marketing Madness to
People-Centered Prosperity*

The conference room was silent as everyone in the room stared at me and my presentation. The usual buzz of laughter and commotion was missing from the room on this sunny afternoon during my C12 core presentation. It was as if the entire group was holding its breath, waiting for me to break the silence.

"Well, I've tried just about everything else," I finally said, exhaling deeply. "Maybe it's time we rethink how we're trying to grow our business."

I looked up from my computer, a skeptical eyebrow raised, and someone from across the room said to me, "I think you should cut your marketing budget…completely."

I looked at him very confused as he continued, "Just like Zappos did…"

DECONSTRUCTING THE NATURE OF CHANGE

Deciding to change is one thing; acting on it requires courage. Could we dismantle the very framework that had sustained our business for years? Even just thinking about it felt like stepping off a cliff. Would we sprout wings before hitting the ground?

Here's the thing about change: once we got going, the belief in our new model solidified. But it didn't happen overnight. It was the product of a continuous cycle of **commitment, courage, growth**, and even more **belief**. Combined, these are the Four Pillars of Change I'd like to share with you.

PILLAR 1: COMMITMENT

During my C12 core presentation, I was introduced to the remarkable story of Zappos, the online shoe retailer that dared to defy conventional wisdom.[2] In the mid-nineties, when buying anything online—let alone shoes—was a novelty, two young entrepreneurs took the plunge into the uncharted waters of e-commerce. No one bought clothes online back then, and the idea of selling shoes without a physical storefront seemed ludicrous. But they were committed.

Fast-forward to the dot-com bubble burst in 2000, and Zappos teetered on the edge of collapse. Sales plummeted, funds dried up, and they faced the harsh reality that many startups did not survive. In a desperate bid to stay afloat, they slashed salaries and staff. Then came the toughest decision of all: eliminating their entire marketing budget.

Imagine that—a company relying on online sales decides to stop marketing online. It was insane and brilliant.

Without the crutch of paid advertising, Zappos doubled down on what they could control: exceptional customer service. They turned every customer interaction into an opportunity to create raving fans.

---

2   Tony Hsieh, *Delivering Happiness: A Path to Profits, Passion, and Purpose* (Grand Central, 2013).

Stories began to circulate—customers calling to order pizza through Zappos, and the company obliging without hesitation. It became like a game, a challenge to see just how far their commitment to service would go.

And it worked. Their sales grew exponentially, fueled solely by word of mouth. They became the gold standard for customer experience, eventually catching the eye of the single largest online retailer, which wanted to purchase them. They made a deal to be acquired for a staggering sum. You might have heard of the retailer, as it continues to be the largest online seller, Amazon.

PILLAR 2: COURAGE

Sitting in that conference room, I felt a kinship with the founders of Zappos. Their story resonated deeply with me. We were at a crossroads in our practice. Despite years of steady business, something felt off. We were spending exorbitant amounts on marketing—seminars, online leads, you name it—but the return on investment was dwindling at best and costing more than I was making at worst. I was sick of the perpetual cycle of bad marketing, bad prospects, and the hope for something better next time around.

"Look," someone said, turning to me as I sat alone in the hot seat during my core presentation. "You've been doing things the same way for years. What if you shifted your focus from chasing new clients to serving the ones you have? What if you invested in a world-class client education and experience?"

I leaned back in my chair, a thoughtful expression on my face. "I'm not sure that is going to work," I admitted. "But it can't be any worse than what I'm doing now."

I nodded slowly and thought for a moment, and said, "I've always believed in putting the client first. Maybe it's time our firm truly lived that out."

Initially, the idea of cutting our marketing budget entirely was too daunting. "Maybe we shouldn't go all in," I suggested during one of our team meetings. I tapped my pen thoughtfully against a notepad. "Perhaps we should start by reducing it incrementally."

I chose to remove our continuing education program for retirees from our marketing budget. It seemed manageable—a slight tightening of the belt rather than a complete overhaul. Yet even that small cut felt like a leap of faith. Without the usual influx of leads from our college classes, I anxiously checked the phone and my email, and looked just about anywhere for activity.

I often would ask the people on our team if we were making a mistake. The very next C12 group, I couldn't wait to bring this topic back up to voice the concerns I wasn't able to shake. They poured into me like they did during my core, and as I took a deep breath, someone shared some advice that I needed to hear.

"Change is always uncomfortable, so just give it some time."

Over the next few months, we continued to shave off portions of the marketing budget—15 percent here, 20 percent there. Each reduction came with its own set of jitters. But with every dollar we saved, we reinvested it directly into enhancing our clients' experience. We upgraded our office space to be more welcoming, produced educational videos exclusively for our clients, and implemented a more personalized approach to customer experience.

One evening, as I prepared to leave the office, I noticed an email from a longtime client named Susan. She wrote about how much she appreciated our planning process called Simplicitree. She stated, "For the first time, I understand my retirement plan! My only regret is not meeting you sooner. Just so you know, I am going to get everyone I care about to become clients of your firm."

I forwarded this email to our team members. "This is why we're doing this," I typed. "Not only does she love us; she wants to tell everyone about us!"

As the months rolled on, the anxiety subsided. We were no longer fixated on the number of new leads but were deeply engaged in enriching the relationships we already had. Our clients noticed the difference. They felt valued, heard, and cared for—not just as accounts but as people.

By the end of the year, we had eliminated our entire marketing budget. The silence that once felt unsettling now felt peaceful. There were no more late nights planning seminars or scrambling to follow up on lukewarm leads. Instead, our days were filled with meaningful interactions and proactive client outreach.

Then something incredible happened. Our phones started ringing—a lot. Clients were referring their friends and family at a rate we'd never seen before.

At one of our advisor study groups, I shared what every advisor loves to talk about: statistics! I shared that our referrals were up 360 percent compared to last year. I could barely contain my excitement.

Here's the best part: we didn't spend any money to get these referrals, not to mention our client retention rate was perfect.

They were talking about us, sharing their experiences, and people were listening. The genuine appreciation we showed our clients was coming back to us in waves.

We realized that by gradually eliminating the noise of aggressive marketing, we allowed the true signal—our commitment to our clients—to shine through. Our courage to change course, little by little, had not only transformed our business but also reaffirmed why we do what we do.

We had not just survived the transition; we had thrived. And all it took was the courage to take that first step and the patience to see it through, one day at a time.

PILLAR 3: GROWTH

As we embraced this new approach, we saw growth in areas we hadn't anticipated. It wasn't just our business that was growing; we were growing personally and professionally.

One of the most transformative changes was how we presented ourselves. I used to wear suits every day, believing it projected professionalism and success. But it never felt like me. One hot summer day, I decided to ditch the suit and wear shorts and a polo shirt to the office. It was a much slower transition than that, but the shock value was totally worth it. However, on one of the early days of my wearing shorts, I had an experience that helped me commit to wearing shorts from that day forward.

"Casual Friday?" a client joked when he walked in.

"Would you rather I wear a suit and fake it or wear what I have on and be true to who I am?" I replied with a grin.

To my surprise, the client relaxed visibly. The conversation flowed more naturally, and the meeting was one of the most productive we'd ever had. It dawned on me that by being authentic, I was giving my clients permission to do the same.

Over time, the office atmosphere shifted. We were still professional—our work ethic and dedication never wavered—but there was a new energy. Clients would come in dressed comfortably, ready to engage in meaningful dialogue rather than stiff formalities.

PILLAR 4: BELIEF

With each positive interaction, our belief in this new model solidified. But this belief didn't emerge overnight; it was the product of a continuous cycle. And with each cycle, our belief in our new approach strengthened even more. This belief wasn't blind faith; it was confidence built on tangible results and personal transformation. It became the anchor that kept us steady, especially during challenging times.

But belief isn't static; it requires nurturing and reinforcement. There were moments of doubt, times when the old ways seemed tempting. During a slow month, the idea of running a seminar or buying leads would creep back in.

"Maybe just one college class," a team member would suggest half jokingly, the glimmer of old habits flickering in his eyes.

I felt the pull too. The allure of quick wins and familiar routines was hard to resist. It was in these moments when the cycle began anew. Our commitment was tested, and we needed the courage to reaffirm our choices.

"Let's think about why we made this change in the first place," I would say, gathering the team. "Remember Susan's email? The look on clients' faces when they truly understand their Simplicitree plan? That's why we're doing this."

We'd revisit the Zappos story, reminding ourselves of how they transformed their business by committing to customer experience over traditional marketing. Their journey mirrored ours, and their success served as a beacon guiding us through our doubts.

This reflection reignited our commitment, empowering us with the courage to push forward. We continued investing in our clients' education and experience, which led to further growth—both in our business and within ourselves. Our belief deepened, becoming an unshakable conviction that we were on the right path.

One afternoon, Kyle shared an insight that encapsulated our journey. "You know," he said, "every time we commit to our clients, muster the courage to do things differently, and see the growth that comes from it, our belief isn't just maintained—it's amplified."

"Exactly," I agreed. "And that amplified belief makes it easier to commit even more deeply. It's a powerful cycle."

We recognized this pattern not just as a sequence of steps but as a dynamic, self-reinforcing loop. Each phase fueled the next: commitment ignites courage; courage fuels growth; growth strengthens belief; belief renews commitment.

As I reflected, I saw how the Four Pillars drove us forward:

- **Commitment** led us to make bold decisions. Everything started with our commitment to change. We weren't just tweaking our business model; we were overhauling it.
- **Courage** enabled us to act on those decisions despite uncertainties. We had to step out of our comfort zones, abandoning the familiar strategies that had once defined our success. Making such a significant shift demanded courage to face uncertainty and the possibility of failure.
- **Growth** emerged from new strategies and strengthened relationships. As we acted on this courage, we experienced growth. This growth wasn't just about our business metrics, but in our understanding of what truly mattered in our work. We saw our clients becoming more engaged, our relationships deepening, and our professional satisfaction increasing. This growth reinforced our initial commitment, making it easier to stay the course.
- **Belief** solidified as we witnessed the positive outcomes, which then deepened our commitment. Our belief was more than just confidence in a business model; it was faith in a philosophy that placed people over profits. It was trust in the idea that by genuinely serving our clients, success would follow.

Following this cycle paid major dividends in our freedoms, which I wrote about in Chapter 1:

- Our **freedom of time** improved as we spent fewer hours chasing leads and more time cultivating meaningful relationships.
- The freedom of choice became evident as we only worked with clients who valued our approach.
- Most importantly, we rediscovered our **freedom of purpose**, aligning our daily work with our core values and passions.

This cycle became the heartbeat of our practice. Each cycle through commitment, courage, growth, and belief fortified our practice's foundation. We became more resilient, adaptable, and confident. We also remained aware that belief requires an ongoing effort. It wasn't a destination but a journey. We had to continuously feed it with positive experiences, client success stories, and personal reflections.

"Belief isn't just something we have," Kevin mused during one of our reflections. "It's something we do. It's an action as much as a feeling."

"Well said," I replied. "And by actively believing and by committing, acting courageously, and embracing growth—we're not just changing our business. We're changing ourselves."

The cycle wasn't merely a business strategy; it was a framework for personal and professional development. It reminded us that every challenge was an opportunity to recommit, to act with courage, to grow, and to strengthen our belief.

By consciously engaging in this cycle, we created a sustainable model that could withstand external pressures and internal doubts. Our belief became a steadfast compass, guiding us through the complexities of running a business in an ever-changing world.

In embracing and articulating this cycle, we didn't just find a new way to operate; we found a new way to thrive. Our journey taught us that belief is both the fuel and the fire—ignited by commitment, stoked by courage, and sustained by growth. It's a continuous process that, when nurtured, leads to extraordinary outcomes.

THE CULTURE OF EXCELLENCE

What we were cultivating was more than a business strategy; it was a culture where "customer experience" wasn't a buzzword but a lived reality. It permeated every aspect of our practice, from greeting clients to handling follow-ups.

We stopped reacting and started anticipating. Instead of waiting for clients to call with questions or concerns, we proactively reached out with insights and updates. We educated them, empowering them to make informed decisions.

Our meetings transformed into collaborative sessions. We weren't there to sell products but to solve problems together. Clients appreciated this approach, and it deepened the trust between us.

THE RIPPLE EFFECT

One afternoon, I received a call from a prospective client.

"I heard from a friend that you helped her not just with her finances but with understanding them," she said. "I want that."

That was the moment I knew we had created something special. Our commitment to excellence was resonating beyond our immediate circle. We weren't just growing a business; we were making an impact.

Reflecting on this, I realized that the Four Pillars—commitment, courage, growth, and belief—weren't just steps but an ongoing cycle. Each feeds into the other, creating momentum that propels you forward.

AN INVITATION

What does this mean for you? Maybe you're where we were—spending time and money on strategies that no longer serve you, feeling stuck in a pattern that's hard to break. It might seem daunting to pivot, to let go of what's familiar.

But I invite you to consider the possibilities. What could happen if you redirected your focus from chasing new clients to truly serving the ones you have? What if you invested in client experience and client education?

It's not easy. It requires commitment and courage. But the growth you'll experience—both personally and professionally—is worth it. And the belief that follows is unshakable.

* * *

As I lock up the office for the day, I glance at the framed quote hanging near the door: "It's not about how much you spend on marketing; it's about how much you invest in people." I smile, knowing the path we've chosen isn't conventional, but it's authentic. In the end, that's what makes all the difference.

CHAPTER 3

THE THREE-DAY FRAMEWORK

Transform Life from Busy to Balanced

The soft glow of my computer screen illuminated my darkened office as I stared at my calendar. It was filled to the brim with back-to-back appointments—client meetings, conference calls—all meticulously color-coded and organized. This digital mosaic was supposed to be a testament to my success as a financial advisor. A full calendar meant a thriving business, right?

Instead of joy, I felt a growing sense of suffocation. Each block of time represented not just an appointment but also a commitment that left me with no room to breathe. There was scarcely any time to do the actual work that these meetings generated—no time to strategize, to plan, or even to reflect.

I leaned back in my chair, rubbing my temples. "Is this really what I worked so hard for?" I muttered to myself.

I had always equated being busy with being successful. The more appointments I had, the more validated I felt. But now, with a calendar so packed, it resembled a game of Tetris. I questioned that assumption. The irony was hard to ignore—I had achieved the busyness I once craved, yet I felt more unfulfilled than ever.

My family was feeling the strain too. Missed dinners and school events and the constant feeling of "I have to take this call" had become all too common. My youngest child had once asked me, "Dad, why are you always talking to other people and not me?" That innocent question just about crushed me.

Something had to change. I couldn't keep up this pace without sacrificing the things that truly mattered.

Determined to regain control over my time, I embarked on a quest to find the best time-management strategies. I devoured books, attended seminars, and experimented with various techniques. But nothing seemed to stick. Each system promised efficiency but often left me feeling just as constrained. Then I developed a system called the Three-Day Framework, which focuses on three types of days: **Play, Preparation,** and **Production.**

SOLVING THE TIME CONUNDRUM

Time management has always been a challenging aspect of my career. In the pursuit of success, I filled every available slot in my calendar with appointments, believing that a fully booked schedule was the hallmark of a top-performing advisor. But as the days blurred together, I realized I was caught in a vicious cycle of endless meetings with little to no time to execute the plans we discussed.

The turning point came one evening when I was reviewing the day's meetings. Despite having met with numerous clients, I felt a nagging dissatisfaction. I hadn't made meaningful progress on any of their plans. Instead, I was merely going through the motions, spreading myself thin, and offering less value than I knew I could provide.

I reached out to one of my buddies, a trusted friend whom I love to share my frustrations with. Sometimes that is the only way I can get through certain situations.

"I have so many appointments, but I feel like I'm not accomplishing anything substantial," I confessed during a late-night call.

I could feel my friend nod sympathetically. "I've been there. It's like running on a treadmill—you're expending energy but not actually going anywhere."

He added, "Maybe it's time to rethink how you're structuring your days. Quantity doesn't always equal quality."

His words resonated with me. I realized my approach needed a fundamental overhaul.

THE THREE TYPES OF DAYS

One evening, after a particularly hectic day of juggling client meetings, strategic planning, and a flurry of emails, I sat down at the kitchen table, exhausted. My wife, Stephanie, was preparing the kids' lunches for the next day, and I noticed how calmly she moved through her tasks.

"How do you stay so organized and unflustered?" I asked her.

Stephanie smiled. "I have my play days with the kids. It keeps me grounded."

"Play days?" I echoed.

"Yes," she explained. "Once a week, I plan a full day of fun activities with the kids—no errands, no chores, just us enjoying time together. It helps me recharge and keeps the kids happy."

Her words struck a chord. Here I was, trying to cram as many tasks as possible into each day, mixing and matching completely different activities—from preparing for meetings to strategizing for the business, and even planning events—all in a futile attempt to be productive. In reality, I was spreading myself too thin, never dedicating enough time to any one task to make meaningful progress.

I realized Stephanie's approach could hold the key to my time management woes. By compartmentalizing her days, she could be fully present in each activity, whether it was a play day with the kids or handling household responsibilities.

Inspired, I began to rethink my schedule. Instead of trying to do everything every day, I decided to categorize my days based on the primary focus. Drawing from various time management strategies and personal insights, I developed a simple yet profound concept: dividing my week into three distinct types of days.

- **Play Days (Red Days):** Days dedicated entirely to rest, relaxation, and rejuvenation—no work allowed. These were my days to spend with family, pursue hobbies, and recharge my batteries.
- **Preparation Days (Yellow Days):** Days spent organizing, planning, and setting the stage for productive work. This included reviewing client information, developing strategies, and handling administrative tasks.
- **Production Days (Green Days):** Focused on client meetings, closing deals, and revenue-generating activities. These were the days to be fully engaged with clients and drive the business forward.

I visualized this system like a traffic light:

- **Red for Stop:** Play Days, where work comes to a complete halt
- **Yellow for Get Ready:** Preparation Days to gear up for action
- **Green for Go:** Production Days to move forward at full speed

Implementing this framework was both exciting and challenging. It required a significant shift in mindset. No longer was I multitasking throughout the day. Instead, I dedicated entire days to a single area of focus. This allowed me to dive deeper into each task without the constant mental gear-shifting that had been draining my energy.

The real challenge, however, was sticking to it. Old habits die hard, and there were times when I was tempted to sneak in a bit of work on a Play Day or mix preparation tasks into a Production Day. But I reminded myself of how ineffective and scattered I felt when I tried to do everything at once.

One particular week stood out. On Monday, a Preparation Day, I spent the entire day organizing client files, developing personalized strategies, and planning for upcoming meetings. On Tuesday and Thursday, my Production Days, I met with clients and focused solely on them, free from the distractions of unfinished prep work. Wednesday and Friday were designated as Play Days. I took Wednesday off to attend my son's school play and spent Friday with my family at the zoo.

By the end of the week, I felt a sense of accomplishment I hadn't experienced in a long time. I was more productive during my working hours and more present during my personal time.

EMBRACE PLAY DAYS

The idea of taking a full day off without any work seemed impossible at first. As a business owner, I felt indispensable. What if a client had an emergency? What if I missed an important opportunity?

I shared my concerns with several of my C12 buddies who are also very close friends.

"Trust me," one of them said. "Taking time off will not ruin your business. It might just save it."

Another one nodded in agreement. "I used to think the same way until I started blocking off time for myself. It made a world of difference."

Taking their advice to heart, I scheduled my first true **Play Day**. I marked it in red on my calendar—a visible reminder that this day was sacred.

When the day arrived, I felt restless. My phone buzzed with notifications, each one tempting me to dive back into work. Frustrated, I took drastic measures. I deleted all work-related apps from my phone—email, calendar, and messaging apps. I informed my team that I would be unreachable and that any emergencies could wait until my return.

With my phone silenced and my mind free from work, I spent the day with my family. The crisp air, the rustling of leaves under our feet, the laughter of my children—it was invigorating. For the first time in a long time, I felt fully present.

That evening, as we gathered around the dinner table, my wife smiled and said, "It's good to have you back."

ATTEND TO PREPARATION DAYS

With Play Days rejuvenating my spirit, I turned my attention to **Preparation Days**. These were the days to organize, strategize, and handle the behind-the-scenes work that often gets overlooked.

I used to think preparation was a waste of valuable time that could be spent on client meetings. But I realized without proper preparation, my Production Days were less effective.

On Preparation Days, I focused on:

- **Reviewing Client Accounts:** Ensuring I am up-to-date on each client's needs and goals
- **Planning Meetings:** Setting clear objectives for upcoming client interactions
- **Developing Tools:** Working on resources like the Simplicitree, TallyFin, or any other ideas I can dream up to enhance client understanding
- **Working on the Business:** Working on my business when I'm not distracted by the business

Many advisors have utilized Preparation Days. Kevin, one of our advisors, meets with his assistant every Monday to go over the week's agenda, prioritize tasks, and make sure everything is in place. It sets the tone for a productive week.

Kyle, who at the time didn't have a dedicated assistant, adjusted the concept to fit his situation. He blocks off Mondays and Fridays for prep work and uses that time to develop snapshots, take care of paperwork, and plan ahead.

MAXIMIZE PRODUCTION DAYS

With Play and Preparation Days enhancing my well-being and organization, my **Production Days** became more focused and productive.

I limited these days to specific times during the week—Wednesdays and Thursdays, from 9:00 a.m. to 4:00 p.m. By narrowing the window, I found I was more engaged during client meetings. I wasn't thinking about the next appointment or an unfinished task. I was fully present.

I also shifted my approach during these meetings. Instead of presenting premade plans, I began **co-planning** with clients. We worked together in real time, using interactive tools to build their financial strategies.

One client remarked, "I feel like I'm truly part of the process now. I understand my plan for the first time in my life."

This collaborative approach not only empowered my clients but also reduced the time I spent preparing outside of meetings.

THE JOURNEY TO BALANCE

Implementing this framework wasn't without its challenges. There were times when I was tempted to squeeze in an extra meeting on a Play Day or skip a Preparation Day to handle an urgent matter.

During one particularly hectic week, I considered reverting to my old habits. Kevin noticed my stress during a study group meeting.

"Remember why you started this," he reminded me. "Burning out won't help you or your clients."

He was right. The Three-Day Framework was more than a scheduling tool—it was a commitment to a balanced life.

Over time, the benefits became undeniable:

- **Increased Productivity:** With focused Production Days, I achieved more in less time.
- **Improved Client Relationships:** Clients appreciated the collaborative approach and my undivided attention during meetings.
- **Enhanced Well-Being:** Regular Play Days reduced stress and increased my overall happiness.
- **Personal Growth:** Preparation Days allowed me to innovate and improve my services continually.

One afternoon, I received an email from a new client, Peter:

"I just wanted to say how much I appreciate your Simplicitree planning process. For the first time, I truly understand my retirement plan. I've told all my friends about you!"

I forwarded the email to a few other advisors to share some excitement with the note, "I love what I do, and so do many of our clients; the more we focus on them, the more they refer back." Let me be clear here. I don't serve my clients to earn referrals, but I certainly love it when they do.

OWNING YOUR TIME

The Three-Day Framework transformed not just my business but my life. I regained control over my time, leading to better performance and deeper satisfaction.

As I shared this approach with other advisors, I realized that while everyone's schedule might look different, the principles remain the same.

- **Set Boundaries:** Protect your Play Days fiercely. Unplug and be present.
- **Prioritize Preparation:** Invest time in planning to make your Production Days more effective.
- **Focus on High-Value Activities:** During Production Days, concentrate on tasks that drive your business forward.

Let me ask, are you feeling overwhelmed or constantly busy without making meaningful progress? I invite you to try the Three-Day Framework.

- **Start Small:** If dedicating entire days feels daunting, begin by blocking off half days.
- **Be Flexible:** Adjust the framework to suit your unique circumstances.
- **Commit:** Stick with it long enough to see the benefits.

One evening, as I sat on the porch watching the sunset, my son joined me.

"Dad, will you come to my game this weekend?" he asked.

"Absolutely," I replied without hesitation.

He smiled, looked back at me, and said, "I'm gonna score three goals for you, Dad!"

Looking back at moments like that confirms why I have stayed true to my priorities and have made the right choices.

CHAPTER 4

THE POWER OF PROACTIVE

*Turn Proactive Client Experience
into Lasting Impact*

The city lights blurred as I sped down the highway, my mind racing faster than my car. It was well past 10:00 p.m., and I was finally heading home after yet another exhausting seminar. The exhilaration of closing deals and acquiring new clients was wearing thin, replaced by a growing sense of emptiness.

As I pulled into the driveway, the house was dark except for a dim light in the kitchen. I quietly opened the door, hoping not to wake anyone. To my surprise, my wife was still up, sitting at the table with what looked like a cup of tea. The leftovers from dinner were neatly packed away, and the silence was deafening.

"How did the seminar go?" she said softly, her eyes reflecting both concern and fatigue.

"Yeah, the seminar ran longer than expected," I replied, avoiding her gaze as I loosened my tie.

She sighed. "You missing dinner is getting very old, and the kids were asking about you."

I felt a pang of guilt. "I know, but these seminars are important for the business. You understand that, right?"

She looked at me intently. "I do, but at what cost? You're missing out on so much—family dinners, bedtime stories, and our lives."

Her words hit me like a ton of bricks. I wanted to protest, to explain I was doing this for us, but deep down, I knew she was right.

Years ago, when I was a rookie financial advisor, my world revolved around numbers and transactions. Success was measured by the volume of clients acquired and the deals closed. My days were a blur of cold calls, back-to-back meetings, and relentless marketing efforts. The chase was exhilarating but also consuming.

I remembered the thrill of landing my first big client, the adrenaline rush of a successful seminar, and the satisfaction of a well-executed marketing program. But as time went on, each achievement felt less fulfilling. The more I chased success, the more it seemed to slip away in areas that truly mattered.

Standing there in the dimly lit kitchen, I saw the toll it was taking—not just on me, but on my family. My wife deserved more than a perpetually absent husband. My children deserved a father who was present, not just a figure who breezed in and out between appointments.

"You can't keep this up," she repeated gently. "We miss you."

I sat down across from her, the weight of her words settling in. "I don't know how to change it," I admitted. "This is what successful advisors do to grow their practice."

She reached out and took my hand. "Maybe there's a different way. Success doesn't have to come at the expense of everything else."

That night, long after she went to bed, I remained at the table, contemplating her words. Could there be another way? Was it possible to achieve success without sacrificing the moments that made life meaningful?

I realized my relentless pursuit of new clients was a never-ending cycle. No matter how many deals I closed, there was always another just out of reach. I was like a hamster on a wheel—running hard but never truly gaining ground.

The next morning, bleary-eyed but resolute, I made a decision. I would find a new path—one that allowed me to be successful in my career without losing myself and my family in the process.

Little did I know that this decision would not only transform my life but would also revolutionize the way I approached my business, leading me to discover the profound difference between customer service and customer experience.

I realized the problem wasn't in chasing clients per se, but in how passively I approached the relationship—reactive instead of proactive. It was time to flip the script and move from simply solving problems to anticipating needs before they ever became a problem. This changed what true success looks like in this business.

THE GREYHOUND SYNDROME

In one of our study groups, Kevin likened the relentless pursuit of new clients to greyhounds chasing a mechanical rabbit around a track—a race with no finish line.

"We're so focused on the chase that we're neglecting the clients we already have," he said.

Kyle chimed in. "It's like we're predators, always hunting but never thinking about planting, cultivating, and nurturing our garden."

Their analogies hit home. We were expending immense energy on attracting new clients—80 percent of our time, by some estimates— while neglecting the gold mine of relationships we had already built.

THE COST OF THE CHASE

I dug deeper into the numbers. We were spending hundreds of thousands of dollars on marketing each year—seminars, online leads, mailers, you name it. Yet the return on investment was dwindling.

I recalled a particularly extravagant seminar we hosted shortly after moving to Charlotte. We rented an upscale venue, mailed out tens of thousands of invitations, and expected a massive turnout. While the initial events drew crowds, over time, attendance dwindled from eighty eager attendees to barely eight.

The realization was stark. The market was saturated, and traditional methods were losing effectiveness.

Moreover, the hidden costs were staggering. Not just the tangible expenses like mailers and meals, but our most valuable resource—time. Each no-show appointment, each lukewarm lead, was time that could have been spent enhancing our services or, more importantly, with our families.

Things have changed over time with virtual appointments, online seminars, online leads, and so on. However, the results are the same. Expensive, exhausting, and very limiting.

FROM REACTIVE SERVICE TO PROACTIVE EXPERIENCE

Sitting in my office one afternoon, I received a call from a longtime client, Mr. Thompson. He sounded frustrated. "I tried logging in to my account, but it's not working," he said. "Can you help me fix this?"

"Of course," I replied, immediately contacting our custodian's IT department to resolve the issue. Within an hour, Mr. Thompson regained access, and he thanked me for the quick assistance.

As I hung up the phone, I realized that while I had provided good customer service by reacting promptly to his problem, I hadn't offered a memorable customer experience. I pondered the difference between the two and how shifting from a reactive approach to a proactive one might have a very profound impact on my business.

CUSTOMER SERVICE: THE REACTIVE APPROACH

Customer service is fundamentally about meeting clients' needs as they arise. It's the backbone of any business—a necessary component that ensures client issues are addressed.

For example:

- **Problem-Solving:** When a client has a problem and calls us to help find a solution, we can respond promptly.
- **Answering Inquiries:** If a client emails with a question about market volatility, we provide a detailed response.
- **Processing Requests:** When a client wants to make adjustments to their Simplicitree plan, we can execute the changes efficiently.

These actions are essential, but they're expected. The client reaches out with a need, and we respond. It's a transactional relationship, much like a firefighter responding to a call—they perform admirably under pressure, but only when summoned.

CUSTOMER EXPERIENCE: THE PROACTIVE TRANSFORMATION

Customer experience is about anticipating needs and creating positive interactions at every touchpoint. It's not just about solving problems. It's about preventing them, getting ahead of them, and adding value in unexpected ways.

A few years ago, I reflected on a personal milestone. When I started Durso Capital, one of the first things I did was purchase a BOSS watch. I shared this story in Chapter 1. It wasn't just a fashion statement. It was a symbol—a reminder that I was now the master of my own time. Owning that watch represented a significant shift in my life, where I took control of my most precious asset.

This personal revelation inspired me to create a meaningful experience for my clients when they reached a similar crossroads. I realized retirement wasn't just the end of a career. It was the beginning of a new chapter—a time when they could transform their past successes into lasting significance.

One of the first clients with whom I shared this inspiration was Tim. After decades of dedication to his family business, Tim was preparing to retire. Rather than simply processing his paperwork and wishing him well—a standard customer service approach—I wanted to commemorate this pivotal moment that was both personal and profound.

I gifted Tim a carefully selected watch, much like the one I had given myself. Along with the watch, I wrote a heartfelt letter, reflecting on his career highlights and the impact he had made in his field. I emphasized how the watch symbolized his newfound control over his time and the opportunities that lay ahead.

In the letter, I wrote:

"The second item is more personal. It should serve as a retirement gift from our family to you. I would like this watch to symbolize God putting you in a position to be the Boss of your time (or even better, God being the Boss of your time!). Wherever you live long term (hopefully Charlotte!), own your time and manage it well!"

I also included the book *Halftime* by Bob Buford. The book explores how individuals can shift from pursuing success to seeking significance in the second half of their lives. I believed its message would resonate with Tim as he contemplated how to invest his time and talents moving forward.

When I presented the gift, Tim was visibly moved. "I didn't expect this," he said, as his eyes glistened. "You've made this transition feel even more special."

A few weeks later, he reached out to me. "I started reading *Half-time*, and it's opened my eyes to so many possibilities," he shared. "I'm excited about what comes next, and I can't thank you enough for your guidance and this thoughtful gift."

By proactively celebrating Tim's retirement in a personalized and meaningful way, I provided an experience that went beyond standard financial advising. I acknowledged not just the end of his working years but the beginning of a journey toward personal fulfillment and legacy.

KEY DIFFERENCES BETWEEN REACTIVE AND PROACTIVE

- Anticipation Versus Reaction
  - *Reactive Service:* Waiting for Mr. Thompson to ask a question about a stock split
  - *Proactive Experience:* Knowing the stock split is going to happen and being proactive in sending the typical FAQs that come up when a stock splits
- Personalization Versus Generalization
  - *Reactive Service:* Answering a client's question about their Simplicitree plan
  - *Proactive Experience:* Interactively reviewing a client's Simplicitree plan alongside them and making the necessary changes required
- Engagement Versus Transaction
  - *Reactive Service:* Processing a withdrawal request promptly
  - *Proactive Experience:* Hosting a webinar on retirement income strategies, providing valuable insights that clients didn't know they needed

IMPLEMENTING PROACTIVE STRATEGIES

Inspired to shift our approach, my team and I brainstormed ways to enhance the client experience:

1. Regular Check-Ins Beyond Reviews
   - We scheduled brief, informal calls just to see how clients were doing—not to discuss finances unless they wanted to. This personal touch showed we cared about them as individuals.
2. Educational Content Tailored to Client Interests
   - Recognizing that clients have diverse interests, we segmented our communications to provide relevant articles, webinars, and resources. For instance, business owners received content on succession planning, while young families got tips on saving for education.
3. Celebrating Milestones
   - We acknowledged important life events. When a client welcomed a new grandchild, we sent a personalized gift. For anniversaries with our firm, we expressed appreciation with handwritten notes.
4. Feedback Mechanisms
   - To continually improve, we regularly meet with our clients and ask for their help in all aspects of our practice. We ask them to tell us what we do wrong and how we can improve, rather than waiting for issues to surface.

THE IMPACT OF PROACTIVE EXPERIENCE

One memorable example of the power of proactive experience involved a client named Michael. He was approaching retirement but hadn't set a firm date. Based on our ongoing conversations, I sensed he was uncertain about the timing.

I reached out and said, "Michael, I've been thinking about your retirement. Would you like to run some scenarios to see how retiring at different times might affect your plans?"

He was grateful for the initiative. "I've been losing sleep over this," he admitted. "I didn't want to bother you until I had made up my mind."

We worked together on his Simplicitree plan to create a very clear picture, giving him confidence in his decision to retire the following year. By anticipating his unspoken concern, I turned a potential source of stress into a positive experience.

WHY PROACTIVE EXPERIENCE MATTERS

- **Deepens Trust:** Clients feel valued when you anticipate their needs, fostering a stronger relationship.
- **Differentiates Your Practice:** In a crowded market, exceptional experiences set you apart.
- **Enhances Satisfaction:** Proactive engagement leads to higher client satisfaction and loyalty.
- **Generates Referrals:** Clients who feel cared for are more likely to refer friends and family, expanding your business organically.

MAKING THE SHIFT

Transitioning from reactive service to proactive experience requires a mindset change:

- **Listen Actively:** Pay attention to clients' life events and concerns, even those not directly related to finances.
- **Think Ahead:** Consider what challenges or opportunities clients might face and offer solutions in advance.
- **Empower Your Team:** Encourage everyone on your team to contribute ideas and take initiative.

- **Invest Time:** While proactive efforts require time up front, they save time in the long run by preventing issues and building stronger relationships.

For our firm, transitioning wasn't easy. It took us three to four years to shift our focus entirely. We phased out expensive marketing campaigns and redirected those funds into client-experience initiatives.

We started small:

- **Personalized Interactions:** We remember birthdays, anniversaries, and significant life events, sending personalized notes or small gifts.
- **Educational Workshops:** Instead of broad seminars for prospects, we hosted intimate workshops for clients on topics they cared about.
- **Proactive Communications:** We reached out regularly, not just when it was time for a review or when the market dipped.

One memorable instance was when I met with a newer client, Mary, whom I helped build her **Simplicitree** plan. The response was overwhelmingly positive.

After her meeting, I walked her back to the lobby. She pulled me aside and said, "I've had a lot of financial advisors in my life, but for the first time, I truly understand my retirement plan!" Her eyes were glistening with excitement, and she continued, "Would you be willing to meet with my parents?"

The results were transformative:

- **Client Retention:** Our attrition rate dropped to less than 1 percent, far below the industry average of 5–10 percent.
- **Referrals:** Without asking, clients referred friends and family at

an unprecedented rate. We went from averaging a few referrals a month to a few referrals a week—every week.

- **Profitability:** Our profits increased, not through aggressive acquisition, but through deepened relationships and increased lifetime value of existing clients.
- **Time Freedom:** With less energy spent chasing new leads, we had more time to focus on what mattered—professionally and personally.

THE VALUE OF TIME

We truly understood the value of our time—not in dollars earned per hour but in the quality of relationships built.

I posed a question to the team: "What's our time worth when we're making a meaningful impact on someone's life?"

Someone responded from the other side of the conference table, "It's priceless."

We recognized by valuing our time and investing it wisely, we enriched our clients' lives and our own.

Our shift from customer service to customer experience wasn't just a business strategy; it was a philosophy. We stopped viewing clients as transactions and started seeing them as relationships to be nurtured. This required us to be proactive, anticipating needs and delivering unexpected value.

One afternoon, I received a call from Peter, a client who had been with us for over a decade.

"I wanted to let you know my sister and her husband are looking to retire," he said. "I told them they had to meet you."

When they came in, Peter's sister shared, "He speaks so highly of you. He says you're not just his advisor but a trusted friend."

Moments like these affirmed our new direction.

One advisor had a client he'd worked with for years who invited him to his daughter's wedding.

"He said I was part of the family," he recalled, beaming. "That's not something that happens when you're just providing a service."

We also redefined success. It wasn't about how many new clients we could acquire but how deeply we could serve the ones we already had.

If you're an advisor spending the majority of your time and resources chasing new clients, I challenge you to reconsider.

- **Evaluate the True Cost:** Consider not just the monetary expenses but the toll on your time and energy.
- **Assess Client Retention:** Are you losing clients due to a lack of engagement or poor service?
- **Measure Impact over Income:** Reflect on the meaningful connections you've made versus the number of deals closed.

BECOMING AN EXPERIENCE-CENTERED ADVISOR

Transitioning to a client-experience-focused model isn't without challenges. It requires a shift in mindset and a commitment to long-term relationships over short-term gains.

But the rewards are immeasurable.

One evening, as I was leaving the office, my phone rang. It was the client who had hugged me during our last meeting.

"I just wanted to thank you again," she said. "You've made such a difference in my life."

As I hung up, I felt a profound sense of fulfillment. This was why I became a financial advisor—not to chase endless leads but to make a lasting impact.

Our journey taught us that the most valuable investment we can make is in our clients' experiences. By focusing on deepening relationships rather than expanding our client base, we found greater satisfaction, loyalty, and profitability.

Part 2

BUILDING THE FUTURE WITH YOUR CLIENTS

CHAPTER 5

THE JOURNEY IS THE DESTINATION

Authentic Connections Create Raving Fans for Life

I still remember the day when a client walked into my office, a hint of skepticism in his eyes and a folder clutched tightly in his hands. Let's call him John. He had been referred by a longtime client of ours, someone who had become more of a friend over the years. As John settled into the chair across from me, he glanced around, taking in the casual atmosphere of our office—no stuffy suits or intimidating boardroom tables here. Just a comfortable space where real conversations happen.

"You're not quite what I expected," he said with a slight grin.

I chuckled. "In a good way?" I responded.

He nodded. "Yeah. I guess I'm used to advisors who are all business with no personality."

That was the moment I knew we were onto something special—not just with John, but with how we approached our entire practice. It wasn't just about managing assets; it was about creating an experience that turned clients into raving fans.

THE FIRST ONE HUNDRED DAYS: UNVEILING THE UNEXPECTED

I thought I had mastered the art of client engagement. After years of reading countless books and meticulously crafting an eight-phase process designed to turn new clients into raving fans within the first one hundred days, I was confident we had it right. This process was a culmination of my experiences and the wisdom gleaned from industry leaders—a foolproof plan, or so I believed.

Eager to validate this, I invited several clients to spend a day at our office. I wanted them to walk through each phase of our process with me, to see it through their eyes and to hear their honest thoughts and reactions. Some had journeyed through all eight phases, while others were still in the early stages of their relationship with us.

The morning sun filtered through the office windows and cast a warm glow on the conference table as we began our session. I was excited, perhaps a bit anxious, to hear how the intentional touchpoints we had so carefully designed were impacting their experiences.

We started with Phase One—the first impression. "Tell me about the moment you first heard of us," I prompted, expecting to hear about our revamped website, an invitation to some event, or how a client raved about us.

"Actually," one client began, "it was your receptionist who made the biggest impression on me. I called to inquire about your services, and she was so genuinely friendly. She made me feel valued before I'd even met you."

Another client chimed in during the discussion of Phase Three—the reaffirmation of their decision. "You know, the most reassuring moment wasn't during any of the formal meetings," he said thoughtfully. "It was when you sent a handwritten note wishing my daughter luck on her college applications. It showed me you cared about more than just my finances."

As we moved through each phase, similar stories emerged. Clients spoke about the small, unplanned gestures—the quick phone call to check in after a market dip, the remembered birthdays, the shared laughter over a misaddressed email—that made them feel truly connected to us.

By midday, a realization dawned on me. The things I thought would stand out—the polished presentations, the comprehensive financial plans, the systematic follow-ups—were not the moments that had the greatest impact. Instead, it was the authentic human interactions, the spontaneous expressions of care, that resonated most deeply with our clients.

Feeling a mix of amazement and frustration, I confessed to the group, "I have to admit, I didn't expect this. We put so much effort into designing this process, thinking those were the things that mattered most."

One client smiled reassuringly and said, "Those things are important, but it's how you make us feel that's unforgettable."

However, what perplexed me the most during this day was when I asked them why they hired me as their advisor. I expected to hear about so many aspects of what we did for our clients—planning, investment strategy, and their experiences—as I'd heard throughout the day. But that is not what I heard. One client sitting up front said, "It was your passion." Another client from the other side of the table quickly followed: "I totally agree with that."

The instant reaction swirling around in my head was something like "Are you serious?" We have so much to offer and do so many things well, and you hired me because I'm passionate? It still frustrates me to this day.

I followed their answer shortly after processing what they were all saying.

I asked, "Why?"

A lone voice from the back of the room said, "If someone is that passionate about what they do, I'm not concerned they are ever going to run off with my money."

Forget the fact I have zero intention to run away with their money. This thought of theirs was driving their decision. That perspective completely changed how I think about clients and what truly matters to them.

By the end of the day, I was humbled and inspired. The feedback was a powerful reminder that in an industry often driven by numbers and strategies, it's the human element that truly makes a difference.

As I reflected on the sessions, I realized the first one hundred days aren't just about implementing a well-crafted process. They're about embracing authenticity, listening more than speaking, and allowing space for genuine connections to flourish, on both sides of the table.

This experience reshaped my approach. I began to see our eight-phase process not as a rigid pathway but as a flexible framework that supports real relationships. It taught me that while planning is essential, we must remain open to the unexpected moments that can have the most profound impact.

I also saw how the first "one hundred days" spills over across a period that's longer than just one hundred days. You'll see this below when you read Phase Six: Annual Review.

Most importantly, as we delve into the journey of transforming clients into raving fans, remember this: it's often the unplanned, sincere gestures that leave the deepest impressions.

The first one hundred days are not just a countdown but an opportunity—a window to show who we truly are and to understand what our clients genuinely value. It's not about perfecting a process. It's about perfecting the art of connection and staying true to who you are while allowing your clients the same courtesy.

PHASE ONE: THE FIRST IMPRESSION–
BEFORE YOU EVEN MEET

Your first impression isn't when they walk into your office or see your smiling face on a Zoom call. It's the moment they first hear about you—whether through your online presence, a referral, or even an ad. This phase might seem out of your control, but it's not. Your responsibility is to set expectations, build trust, and make sure potential clients know you're the right fit for them.

In today's digital age, clients will do their research. They'll Google you, read reviews, and check out your website. If what they find doesn't meet a certain standard, you might lose them before you even know they were interested. It's crucial to have an intriguing, unique message that makes people want to take the next step.

I used to put so much time and effort into the story our office told because I believed that a first impression would make all the difference. Now, don't get me wrong; that impression is important, but it's not your first impression. Your last impression may matter way more to clients and your future referrals. The next time you interact with a client may set the stage for how they speak about you when a trusted friend asks them whom they work with.

This perspective shift has made a huge difference with our team and the overall impact on the referrals we receive.

PHASE TWO: RECOGNIZING THEIR NEED–
HELPING CLIENTS SEE THEIR SHORTFALL

Clients often come to us because they sense something isn't right, even if they can't put their finger on it. Our role isn't to sell them a product but to help them identify and understand their problems.

We use a tool called Simplicitree, which helps visualize their financial situation, particularly their "shortfall." It's the gap between their desired future income and what they have right now. When clients see their shortfall laid out in clear terms, it's often an eye-opening experience.

For example, a couple came in thinking they were on track for retirement. By walking them through Simplicitree, they realized they had a $2,000 monthly shortfall. "This is why we haven't been sleeping well," they admitted. It wasn't about selling them an annuity or an investment product. It was about educating them on their income shortfall and together figuring out how to fix it. More on the shortfall later (hint: Chapter 7).

PHASE THREE: REAFFIRMING THEIR DECISION–OVERCOMING BUYER'S REMORSE

Remember John, the client I mentioned earlier? After our initial meeting, even though he was enthusiastic, I knew he'd probably experience some doubt—that classic buyer's remorse. It's human nature to question the important decisions we all make, especially significant ones involving our financial future.

Our job is to reaffirm their decision, not by pushing a sale but by continuing to build trust and providing value. We help clients take ownership of their financial plans by involving them in the process with Simplicitree. Instead of handing them a prepared plan, we build it together, ensuring they understand each aspect of the current financial situation and what they can expect in the future.

John later told me, "You're the first advisor who didn't make me feel like I was being sold something. You were the first financial advisor I've ever had allow me to be a part of the planning process. All the others presented what they recommended, and I didn't realize it until I started working with you. So thank you for allowing me to co-plan with you!"

That's the goal—to move from a transactional relationship to a collaborative one.

PHASE FOUR: ONBOARDING—YOUR SECOND CHANCE AT A FIRST IMPRESSION

Onboarding is where many advisors drop the ball. Once the paperwork is signed, they move to the next prospect. But onboarding is your second chance to make a first impression—a lasting one.

We make the onboarding process memorable by setting clear expectations and making clients feel welcomed and valued. It's not just about getting their accounts set up. It's about integrating them into our community.

I often think of onboarding like inviting someone into your home for the first time. You wouldn't just open the door and walk away, leaving them to figure everything out themselves. You'd take their coat, offer them a seat, get them a drink, and make sure they're comfortable. Inviting someone into your home is no different than onboarding a client to your firm.

The reason I believe this is your second chance at a first impression is because they've never been a client before, so what you do when they become one definitely qualifies as a first impression. Make that impression count!

PHASE FIVE: CONTINUING EDUCATION— EMPOWERING CLIENTS THROUGH KNOWLEDGE

Education is at the heart of what we do. We believe an informed client is an empowered client. If you ever talk to a real estate broker, what do you think their answer would be if you asked, "What's the most important thing I need to know about real estate?" Drumroll, please—location, location, location. The next time someone asks you what's the most important thing you need to do as a financial advisor, your answer would be to—educate, educate, educate.

We hold client-only workshops, send out relevant and personalized emails, and even produce several podcasts and videos to keep our clients informed about market trends, investment strategies, and financial planning.

One of our advisors, Kevin, excels at this. He holds sessions to help clients understand their statements and navigate online portals. "By the time we're done," he says, "clients often tell me it's the first time they truly understand their investments."

This continuing education builds confidence and trust. When the market fluctuates, our clients aren't panicking; they're calling to ask if now is a good time to invest more.

PHASE SIX: THE ANNUAL REVIEW— CONNECTING THE DOTS

Wait…annual review? I thought this was just the first one hundred days. It is, and it's important to make the annual review part of this conversation.

First, no annual review should ever *just* be about reviewing numbers, high-fiving for good years, and figuring out how to make up for bad ones. Nor should an annual review be a routine check-in. As far as I'm concerned, the annual review is an opportunity to connect *all* the pieces of a client's financial puzzle. At our firm, we revisit their Simplicitree plan, update their financial data, and show them how far they've come.

Here's the thing: have you ever heard of the forgetting curve?[3] It's a study that suggests that people forget about 50 percent of new information within an hour of learning it, 70 percent within twenty-four hours, and 90 percent within a week unless they actively review or apply the information. This is not good news for people in our line of work. It effectively means your annual reviews are not annual reviews at all. Instead, you're starting over again. Even if that's the last

---

3　See Hermann Ebbinghaus, *Memory: A Contribution to Experimental Psychology* (Martino Fine Books, 2011).

thing you want to hear, don't worry. You *should* still walk each client through the process. Before you do, be sure to give clients the tools they need to *see* the entire year, or even farther back…and to follow along throughout the year.

Our firm developed a tool called TallyFin, which allows us to share a Snapshot to illustrate historical performance and income growth. Clients are often amazed to see how their dividends have increased over time, contributing to their financial goals. Our Snapshots show their entire history going back to the day they started with us and highlight four major areas: **deposits, withdrawals, dividend income**, and **value** for each year they have been a client. This complete historical visualization is a great way to share the true value story of what you do for your clients.

I remember a client who came in with her statements meticulously marked up. She was so engaged that she practically led the review herself. "I feel like I'm finally in control of my financial future," she said. That's the kind of ownership we strive for.

PHASE SEVEN: TAKING OWNERSHIP–
CLIENTS AS PARTNERS

When clients take ownership of their financial plans, magic happens. They come to meetings prepared, they ask insightful questions, and they become active participants in their financial journey.

It's not uncommon for clients to bring in new ideas or even challenge us on certain assumptions. We welcome it. It means they're engaged and invested—both literally and figuratively.

I often ask clients, "If you are not vested in your future, how could you trust me with it?" Your clients need to have as much ownership of their plan as you do. They need to not only understand it, but also understand why you are recommending the investment strategy they are using. If they take ownership, your referrals will go up.

It's crazy to me that the more someone owns something, the more they want to tell everyone about it. Let that sink in. If your clients own their plan and their investment strategy, you will reap the benefits of more referrals.

We'll come back to the topic of clients as partners in Chapter 6.

PHASE EIGHT: THE ENGAGED GROUPIE– CREATING RAVING FANS

The final phase is when clients become advocates for your business without you asking. They refer friends and family because they genuinely believe in the value you provide for a few reasons. They understand their plan, they know why they are using their investment strategy, and they own all of it. You are just the guide. You are Yoda, and they are Luke Skywalker. You are Merlin, and they are King Arthur. You are Morpheus, and they are Neo. Get the picture?

We don't have to ask for referrals. They come naturally. One client told me, "I wish my CPA cared about me as much as you do." It's the highest compliment we can receive.

THE AUTHENTIC ADVISOR–BEING TRUE TO YOURSELF

Throughout this entire journey, authenticity is key. Clients can sense when you're putting on an act. I show up to meetings in attire that's comfortable for me—sometimes in flip-flops, often looking like I just came off the golf course. It's not about being unprofessional; it's about being genuine.

"You're not like other advisors," a client once told me. "And that's a good thing." By being ourselves, we create an environment where clients feel comfortable being themselves too. Don't be afraid to allow the real you to show up in all your prospect and client interactions.

Creating raving fans isn't about implementing a slick marketing strategy or following a rigid script. It's about guiding clients through a journey—one that starts before you even meet them and continues long after they've signed on the dotted line.

It's about educating, empowering, and engaging them every step of the way. When you do that, not only do you transform their lives, but you also transform your practice.

As I reflect on John's journey from a skeptical newcomer to a raving fan, I'm reminded why we do what we do. It's not just about managing wealth. It's about enriching lives.

CHAPTER 6

OWNERSHIP CHANGES EVERYTHING

Turn Prospects into Clients with Co-Planning

When I was in high school, my world revolved around sports. While my athletic abilities caught the attention of several colleges, my academic performance was pretty average. Still, I was recruited by numerous schools, each offering me the chance to play sports at the next level. I chose a college and accepted an athletic scholarship, believing my path was set.

During my first week on campus, something unexpected happened. I felt a profound spiritual tug—a conviction that made me question the direction of my life. One night, I woke up in a cold sweat as if God was asking me, "Whom are you going to serve? You can only serve one master. Will it be sports or me?" The question weighed heavily on my heart. After much prayer and a hard conversation with my coach, I made a difficult decision. I walked away from my scholarship and quit the team.

Suddenly, I found myself in uncharted territory. Without the scholarship, I was responsible for paying my tuition. I vividly remember the shock of receiving that first bill. The numbers stared back at me, a stark reminder of the financial burden I had willingly shouldered. I had to find a job immediately to make ends meet. The reality of my situation hit me like a ton of bricks.

With no sports to fall back on and lacking strong academic foundations, I faced an uphill battle. But something remarkable happened: I took ownership of my education because I suddenly had a vested interest in my schooling, since I was paying for it. Every class, every assignment, every exam mattered in a way they never had before. I was no longer just getting by. I was actively engaged in my learning and focused on building a future for myself.

Here's a fundamental truth I learned: ownership changes everything. When you don't own something—when you haven't invested in it personally—it doesn't hold the same value. It's easy to be indifferent or disengaged. But when you have a stake in the outcome, you become committed. You care deeply about the results because they directly affect you.

This lesson extends far beyond personal education and applies to the world of financial planning. In my years as a financial advisor, I've observed a recurring pattern. First, clients often don't take ownership of their financial plans. Then they rely entirely on their advisors to create and manage their plans. The advisor presents recommendations, and the client agrees with a simple nod. There's little engagement and little personal investment in the process.

When things go off the rails—as they sometimes do—and the client becomes dissatisfied, they blame the advisor, fire them, and move on to the next professional, hoping for better results. The cycle repeats itself with each new advisor owning the plan and the client remaining a passive participant.

Without ownership, the client's relationship with their financial future remains superficial. Breaking this cycle requires a shift in approach.

Clients need to take ownership of their financial plans just as I took ownership of my education. When they do, everything changes. They become actively involved in the planning process, understanding the strategies and decisions being made. They have a vested interest in the outcomes because they've contributed to the creation of the plan. But what *is* ownership in this scenario? Is it just about the money they contribute to their funds? Or is it something else? Let's take a look.

OWNERSHIP STARTS WITH CO-PLANNING

Ownership starts when you add an aspect of co-planning into the equation. This was one of the most transformative practices we've ever added to our firm. We did this with the help of a planning system I've mentioned several times now, Simplicitree (more on this below). Instead of crafting financial plans behind closed doors and presenting them to clients as a finished product, we involve clients directly in the planning process from the very beginning.

Here's a glimpse of how things play out in our practice today.

THE FIRST MEETING: JUMPING RIGHT IN

When clients—whether new or existing—come into our office or join us online, we get straight to the point. Gone are the days when we'd spend twenty or thirty minutes on small talk, trying to build rapport. Now, after a brief greeting—perhaps a comment about the weather—we dive right into the planning process.

Some might think this approach is abrupt, but we've found that clients appreciate the efficiency. They're not here to make friends; they're here to secure their financial future.

STARTING WITH A BLANK SLATE

When we open our Simplicitree software, it's completely blank. That's intentional. We don't prefill any information or make any assumptions. We want the client to see this is *their* plan, built with *their* input, and we're merely facilitators in the process.

HANDING OVER THE CONTROLS

We hand the client a wireless keyboard, or if we're meeting virtually, we give them control over the screen. This physical act of giving them the tools reinforces the idea they are in control.

I remember one meeting where a client looked surprised when I handed him the keyboard. "You want me to do it?" he asked.

"Absolutely," I replied. "This is your plan. Let's build it together." From that moment on, that client and many after him have been taking ownership of their Simplicitree plan.

THE FIVE KEY AREAS

From there, we guide them through five major categories:

1. **Retirement Date:** When do you want to retire?
2. **Lifestyle Needs:** How much income do you need to live on in retirement?
3. **Life Events:** Any significant expenses coming up—like a wedding, home renovations, or a new car?
4. **Investments:** What accounts do you currently have? Let's add them one by one.
5. **Income Sources:** Do you have any residual income, pensions, or Social Security benefits?

As they input their information, the clients become actively engaged. They often say things like "I have a 401(k) with Fidelity—let me log in and get the exact amount" or "I forgot about that old mutual fund. Let's include that too." Before I did this type of interactive co-planning, I often had a hard time getting a clear picture of a prospect's entire financial situation. That is no longer the case.

REAL-TIME ADJUSTMENTS

One of the powerful aspects of this approach is the ability to make real-time adjustments. For instance, I had a client couple who mentioned they wanted to add a pool to their home, renovate their kitchen, and move the laundry room downstairs—all totaling about $140,000. We added these life events into the plan right in front of them in seconds.

They were amazed at how quickly we could see the impact. "Wow," they said, "we can see immediately whether this makes sense for us financially."

BUILDING RAPPORT NATURALLY

As we go through the plan, personal stories and insights often emerge. When discussing life events, clients might share their dreams and concerns. This opens the door to deeper conversations.

For example, when a client mentions they're planning a big trip or considering early retirement, we can explore those ideas together. This organic rapport building is far more effective than forced small talk at the beginning of the meeting.

WHEN CLIENTS TAKE OWNERSHIP

Clients often become so invested in the process that they want everything to be precise. I've had clients log in to their accounts during the meeting to get up-to-the-minute balances. "Hold on," they'll say. "I want to make sure we have the exact number."

In one memorable instance, a client emailed me after our meeting to update a 401(k) balance that had changed slightly in the two weeks since he had last checked. He wanted his plan to reflect the most current data.

TRANSPARENCY BUILDS TRUST

Starting with a blank screen and building the plan together eliminates any sense of a hidden agenda. Clients can see there are no behind-the-scenes manipulations—everything is out in the open.

This transparency mirrors the way CPAs work with their clients, asking detailed questions and filling out forms together. By adopting a similar approach, we elevate the level of trust in our relationships.

Said another way, if we are the Wizard of Oz, we are allowing the prospect and client to see behind the curtain. No more secrets or between-meeting planning. This co-planning approach has changed just about everything for our clients and opens the door for them to take ownership of their Simplicitree plan and investment strategy.

OVERCOMING INITIAL HESITATIONS

Some advisors worry that clients might be reluctant to share detailed financial information up front. But we've found the opposite to be true. When clients see the plan is blank and they have control, they're more open to sharing all their information.

Of course, there are moments when clients might feel embarrassed or uncertain. In those cases, we reassure them. "This is your plan. You can include as much or as little information as you like. The more complete your plan is, the better it will help you make decisions for your future."

PERSONALITIES IN PLAY

Every advisor brings their style to the process. Some are more analytical, while others are more conversational. Co-planning allows for these differences while maintaining a client-focused approach.

During the meeting, clients often pick up on our body language and expressions. I've had clients say, "I noticed you made a face—what does that mean?" This opens the door for honest conversations about their financial situation. These honest conversations are what I like to call truth telling. More on that later.

In one humorous instance, a client caught me off guard when she said, "Why did you make that look just now?" I hadn't realized I had reacted visibly. It was a moment that deepened our connection and allowed for candid discussion about the concerns I had about her plan and the potential danger of failure.

THE CLIENT BECOMES THE ADVISOR

By giving clients control, we flip the traditional dynamic. They become active participants, even taking on a quasi-advisor role as they navigate the software. This shift empowers them and heightens their engagement.

At the same time, they begin to understand the complexities of financial planning. They see firsthand how different variables affect their outcomes, which enhances their appreciation for our expertise.

As clients immerse themselves in the planning process, their real concerns come to the surface. They may express fears about not being able to retire when they want or worries about affording significant expenses.

By addressing these concerns in real time, we can adjust the plan accordingly. If retiring at sixty-five doesn't seem feasible, we can explore alternatives together.

I once worked with a client who wasn't sure if he could ever retire. He said, "That's why I'm here—to find out if it's even possible." By inputting his financial information together, we discovered that with some adjustments, retirement was indeed within reach. The relief on his face was amazing.

THE EVOLUTION OF SIMPLICITREE

Today, Simplicitree involves clients deeply in the planning process. It helps them understand their financial landscape and empowers them to make informed decisions. However, if I've made our shift toward co-planning seem like it was easy, it wasn't. Nor was it an overnight decision.

Initially, we experimented with sending questionnaires for clients to fill out in advance. But we realized this method didn't foster the engagement we were looking for.

We then had clients fill out questionnaires in the lobby before the meeting. But even that felt impersonal. Then we would fill out the questionnaire together with them in the meeting, but this, too, wasn't having much of an impact.

Then, in a crazy twist, I bought a touch screen monitor (one of those fifty-five-inch wall-mounted ones), and while I was presenting Simplicitree, a client noticed an issue with his plan, so I changed it right then and there. He asked if he could make some more changes, and I took notice. That was the moment when I decided I would start building Simplicitree plans together, right in front of the prospect.

Where Simplicitree is concerned, we didn't set out to build a planning system that helps clients take ownership of their plan. However, it played out that way, and I'm thankful for it. While it may not be the most feature-rich or complex planning tool on the market, it excels in one crucial area: fostering client engagement.

I noticed when prospects rolled up their sleeves and got involved in their planning process, they became clients. This was the beginning of what we now call the transformative power of co-planning. Within the first twenty minutes of the meeting, we've often completely changed the narrative of the client-advisor relationship. Prospects move from being guarded and uncertain to engaged and empowered.

TAKING OWNERSHIP CHANGES EVERYTHING

Today, when clients take ownership of their financial plans through Simplicitree, they're more committed to the strategies we develop together. If adjustments are needed, they're invested in finding solutions rather than assigning blame. The relationship becomes a true partnership, with both advisor and client working. They gain a sense of ownership over their financial futures, with a clear understanding of where they stand and what steps they need to take.

Just as paying for my education transformed my attitude toward learning, encouraging clients to take ownership of their financial plans transforms their relationship with their finances. It's a powerful shift that leads to better outcomes and a more fulfilling planning experience.

By embracing transparency, fostering engagement, and empowering clients to take an active role, we not only break the cycle of client disengagement but also elevate the practice of financial advising.

I'm going to stay with Simplicitree in the next chapter to help you see several ways you can implement co-planning in your practice.

CHAPTER 7

EMBRACE THE SHORTFALL

Financial Gaps Motivate Clients to Change

When I ran my first marathon in my mid-thirties, I thought, "Hey, I was a great athlete in high school, I played college soccer, and I've always been fast. How hard could it be?" Running 26.2 miles sounded tough, but with the speed and endurance I used to have, I figured I'd be cruising to the finish line, waving at everyone as I passed them like some kind of running deity.

To train, I woke up at 5:00 a.m., ran in the cold, in the rain, even on days when the only thing I felt like running was a hot bath. (If you know me, you know how ridiculous that would be.) I had playlists, fancy running shoes, and a diet plan that made me dream of a future where pasta wasn't my best friend. I was determined to finish well and imagined crossing the finish line with my arms raised, like Rocky, while the crowd erupted in cheers.

Race day came. I was pumped. The first few miles were great. I was weaving through runners, nodding at spectators, feeling like I was back on the soccer field. Around mile ten, I thought, "I've got this. I'm a machine." By mile fifteen, I wondered if I'd ever see my toes again. By mile twenty, I'd forgotten why I wanted to do this in the first place. By mile twenty-three, I was having deep, philosophical debates with myself about why humans ever decided to walk upright.

Finally, I hit mile twenty-six. My legs were moving purely out of habit at this point; my mind was somewhere between delirium and divine intervention. As I approached the finish line, the crowd started to cheer louder. "This is it!" I thought. "This is my moment!"

And then, out of the corner of my eye, I saw her—a very pregnant woman, maybe eight months along, gracefully gliding past me like she was out for a Sunday stroll. I was barely holding it together, every step a new negotiation with my body, yet here she was, overtaking me with a smile on her face like she was enjoying a scenic tour of the city.

I pushed harder, but let's be real: my *push* at that point was more of a desperate shuffle. We crossed the finish line, and there's a picture to prove it: me, sweaty, exhausted, looking like I'd just crawled out of a swamp, and her, beaming, baby bump and all, fresh as a daisy. I'm not sure who was prouder in that photo—her for crushing it or me for surviving.

As humbling as it was, it was also a reminder: no matter how much you train or how fast you used to be, life often tells you speed isn't everything. If you're going to get beat by someone, it might as well be by a true superhero—someone running for two.

That race taught me another important lesson: there's a gap between where you *think* you are and where you actually are. I thought I was still that speedy, unstoppable athlete from my younger days, ready to conquer any physical challenge with ease. But reality, with its humbling clarity, reminded me I had a lot more work to do to get to where I wanted to be.

KNOWING THE SHORTFALL

This same concept of "shortfall" applies to financial planning, especially in Simplicitree. It's the difference between where you are and where you want to be financially. Like me, standing at the starting line thinking I'd cruise through that marathon, many people believe they're on track to meet their financial goals. But when we dig into the details, we often find a gap—a shortfall—between their current financial position and the destination they're aiming for. This shortfall is typically the reason they are there in the first place, but they couldn't put their finger on it until they saw it visualized in Simplicitree.

This shortfall almost always shows up as an income gap. In Simplicitree, it's visualized in red so you can't miss it. Just as I realized I wasn't as prepared for the marathon as I'd thought, clients might find they're not as financially prepared for their future as they'd hoped. And that's okay! The important thing is recognizing your shortfall and then creating a plan to solve it. A quick sidenote: solving for solutions is much more impactful than making assumptions. More on that later.

In the marathon of life, whether you're trying to cross the finish line of retirement, buy a home, or achieve financial freedom, it's not just about the speed you start with but about having the right plan, pace, and strategy to get to the end successfully. Because while it's humbling to get passed by a pregnant woman in a race, it's even more sobering to learn you're not as close to your financial goals as you thought.

UNDERSTANDING THE CLIENT'S SHORTFALL

In financial planning, the concept of shortfall is a lot like that moment in the marathon when you realize you're not as close to the finish line as you thought you'd be. It's the difference between where your clients are and where they want to be. Recognizing and addressing this gap is crucial for both you and your clients. It's not just about numbers; it's about emotions, expectations, and the journey toward financial security.

Just as I had to adjust my expectations and push through to the end of that marathon, clients need to understand their financial shortfall and make the necessary adjustments to reach their goals. It's about preparing for the long haul, pacing themselves, and making sure they have the right support to cross the finish line, stronger and more confident in their financial future.

THE BASE PLAN: A DIAGNOSTIC TOOL

When I entered the financial advisory field, my focus was primarily on assets—what clients had, where the weaknesses were, and how I could motivate them to invest with me. It was like being a mechanic who only cared about selling new parts rather than understanding why the car wasn't running smoothly. I'd assess their portfolio, find flaws, and think, "How can I get them to sell their current investments and buy into mine?" While I genuinely believed in what I recommended, my approach lacked a holistic perspective.

Over time, I realized that clients don't need another sales pitch; they need a roadmap. And you can't chart a course to a destination without knowing the starting point. You can't plan for the future if you don't know where you are right now.

That's where the Base Plan in Simplicitree comes into play. We created the Base Plan because we needed a starting point—a foundation upon which to build a tailored financial strategy. Surprisingly, this critical step is often missed in our industry. Advisors frequently jump straight into recommending products or complex strategies without fully understanding the client's current situation.

The Base Plan is a simple, strategy-free snapshot of the client's financial life. It's not about deep-diving into their investments or dazzling them with intricate models.

Instead, we straightforwardly organize their assets, focusing on clarity and simplicity. We categorize investments into "aboveground" and "belowground" assets—a concept I'll delve into shortly.

The primary purpose of the Base Plan is to diagnose the problem by identifying the client's shortfall—the gap between where they are and where they want to be. Just like a doctor wouldn't prescribe medication without first diagnosing the ailment, we shouldn't recommend financial solutions without understanding the client's current financial health.

In many ways, the Base Plan is like a diagnostic test for a car that's not running well. Before you can fix the problem, you need to know what's wrong. The Base Plan strips away the complexities and provides a clear, honest assessment of the client's financial situation. It's not about judgment or criticism; it's about understanding.

By starting with the Base Plan, we ensure the client is fully engaged in the process. They provide the information, they see the data laid out plainly, and they understand the challenges they face. Again, this involvement is crucial because it fosters ownership. The client isn't being told what to do; they're part of the discovery process.

Unfortunately, many financial advisors overlook this essential step. They focus on risk assessments, asset allocations, or product pitches without establishing where the client currently stands. It's like trying to give directions when you don't know where you are—inefficient at best and misleading at worst.

In our practice, we emphasize the Base Plan because it sets the stage for meaningful planning. We acknowledge that before we can chart a course to the future, we must understand the present in all its nuances. Only then can we develop strategies that are truly tailored to the client's needs and goals.

By simplifying the complex and visualizing the challenges, we empower clients to take ownership of their financial journey. They see, often for the first time, where they truly stand financially. They understand their shortfall and are motivated to find a solution to fill in the gap. This approach not only builds trust but also fosters a collaborative relationship where the client feels confident and informed.

ABOVEGROUND AND BELOWGROUND INVESTMENTS

Early in my career, I learned the importance of asset allocation. I would often use what I learned to show value to my clients with complicated charts and terminology. Over the years, I have adjusted how I believe and think about asset allocation. Most importantly, I don't feel the need to show value here and truly want to simplify asset allocation by categorizing investments into just two types:

1. **Belowground Investments:** Think of these as the roots of a tree—bank-backed, government-backed, or insured investments. They're protected but not entirely risk-free. After all, every investment carries some level of risk.
2. **Aboveground Investments:** These investments are everything else—stocks, corporate bonds, real estate, and so on. They aren't protected by banks or government institutions, and they carry higher volatility.

This straightforward classification helps clients easily understand where their assets stand without getting lost in the jargon of Wall Street.

VISUALIZING THE SHORTFALL

Once we've organized their assets, we introduce them to their shortfall. We use simple graphs and charts to illustrate the gap between their desired lifestyle income and their base income sources, like Social Security or pensions.

Imagine their faces when they see a chart dominated by a glaring red section—it's like watching someone realize they've been walking around with their underwear on the outside of their pants all day. That red represents their shortfall, and it's an emotional moment. They start to grasp the reality of their situation.

LETTING REALITY SINK IN

At this point, silence is golden. Resist the urge to jump in with solutions or reassurances. Let them process what they're seeing. It's uncomfortable, yes, but necessary. This moment of realization is where ownership begins.

I often compare it to parenting. As a parent, there are often times when it's so obvious to see the problem in your child, and for some reason, they are completely incapable of seeing it themselves. This is one of those moments, but this time they can see it and easily understand it. That's the power of Simplicitree.

Getting my kids to take responsibility for a mess they've made or a problem they have or understand their immature behavior is infinitely harder than running a business. Similarly, clients need to own their financial challenges before they can overcome them. They need to feel the weight of that shortfall.

Eventually, the client will break the silence with the million-dollar question, "How do we fix it?" This is the turning point. They've acknowledged the gap and are seeking guidance. They're not looking for a superhero to swoop in and save the day. They want a guide to help them navigate the path ahead. If a prospect asks an advisor how they could help fix their shortfall, the advisor has just made a client.

It's that moment in life when someone realizes they can't do it alone and need help. They don't just need the help, they want it, and in this instance, the advisor is the one they want to get it from.

INTRODUCING RETIREMENT RATES

Now that the client is engaged and ready to take action, we introduce them to the three key rates in Simplicitree:

1. **Retirement Rate:** The rate of return they need to achieve to ensure they don't run out of money by their life expectancy
2. **Preservation Rate:** The rate required to maintain their current amount of assets until the end of their life expectancy
3. **Legacy Rate:** The rate needed to leave a specific legacy dollar amount to heirs and/or charities

For example, if a client needs an average return of 2.5 percent to meet their retirement goals by depleting all their assets at their life expectancy age, that's their Retirement Rate. Seeing these concrete numbers helps clarify the path forward. This is where Simplicitree stands out in the financial planning crowd. Most planning software programs offer assumption-based planning, where the entire plan is based on an assumed rate of return. Simplicitree solves for what clients need in these three scenarios.

While assuming a rate of return may seem intuitive based on a client's risk tolerance, solving for a rate of return will give an advisor a greater sense of the appropriate risk the client may need to take to solve their shortfall.

THE CLIENT AS HERO

Clients must see themselves as the heroes of their own financial stories. We're just the guides—the Yodas to their Luke Skywalkers. By understanding their shortfall and the rates required to overcome it, they become empowered to make informed decisions and take ownership of their plan and the investment strategy that solves their shortfall.

As advisors, it's tempting to rush in with solutions. We see the problem, and we know how to fix it. But remember, this isn't about us. It's about them. Give them space to absorb the information. Let them ask questions. Be patient.

Skipping over this critical phase can lead to misunderstandings and buyer's remorse. Clients might agree to a plan without fully grasping it, only to backtrack later when uncertainty creeps in.

AVOIDING THE RISK-FIRST PITFALL

Many advisors make the mistake of leading with risk assessments. They hand over a risk questionnaire, categorize the client, and build a portfolio based on that without ever addressing the shortfall. This is like a doctor prescribing medication without diagnosing the illness.

In Simplicitree, we prioritize understanding the client's goals and the gap they need to bridge, which is their shortfall. Only then do we consider the appropriate level of risk to achieve those goals.

By taking clients through a logical, step-by-step process, we ensure they're involved at every stage. They help build their plan, understand their shortfall, and participate in crafting the solution. This collaborative approach not only educates them but also builds trust and confidence.

CLOSING THE GAP

Remember my marathon story? Just like I realized too late that my training hadn't quite prepared me for the full 26.2 miles, many clients are unaware of their financial gaps until they're deep into the race and struggling to keep up. Our role is to help them recognize and address these shortfalls before they become overwhelming and keep them up at night.

By simplifying the complex, visualizing the challenges, and empowering clients to take ownership, we help bridge the gap between where they are and where they want to be. In doing so, we not only guide them toward achieving their financial goals, but we also become true partners in their journey toward financial security.

The next time you sit down with a client, resist the urge to be the hero who tries to carry them to the finish line. Instead, hand them the map, point out the obstacles, and run alongside them as they chart their course. After all, it's their race—we're just here to help them cross the finish line strong and victorious.

CHAPTER 8

HAUNTED HOUSES

*Prioritize Client Needs over Their
Emotion Toward Risk*

A few years ago, my wife and I decided to brave the thrills of SCa-rowinds—a theme park that transforms into a labyrinth of haunted houses and spine-chilling attractions every Halloween season. We went with friends. One of them, Lisa, was absolutely terrified of haunted houses. The mere thought of entering one made her knees buckle. At first, I thought she was just kidding around, but the longer the night went on, the more I realized she was genuinely scared.

As we queued up for the first haunted house, Lisa clung to her husband's back like a backpack, eyes squeezed shut, refusing to peek even for a second. Meanwhile, I strolled through the dimly lit corridors, thoroughly enjoying the theatrics. I knew the "monsters" were just underpaid actors in makeup and the chainsaw-wielding maniac was probably Steve from accounting, blowing off steam.

Sometimes I would walk into one of the houses or rooms backward so I could watch Lisa freak out. It was more entertaining to watch her in fear than it was to see if I could be scared by something.

I was so distracted by her fear and the amusement of it that I was never even close to being afraid.

Watching Lisa's reaction, I realized how subjective risk is. Here we were, experiencing the exact same environment, yet our perceptions couldn't have been more different. For me, it was all in good fun—a controlled setting designed to thrill but not harm. For Lisa, it was a real-life nightmare.

This experience got me thinking about how we perceive risk in the financial world. Just like Lisa and I did in that haunted house, clients and advisors often have vastly different perspectives on risk. Risk is not a one-size-fits-all concept; it's deeply personal and incredibly hard to pin down. And when it comes to money, risk can be broken down into two very different categories: **emotional risk** and **needs risk**.

THE ILLUSION OF CONTROL: EMOTIONAL RISK VERSUS NEEDS RISK

Financial advisors often get trapped in our version of a haunted house—obsessed with charts, market trends, and compliance checklists. We focus on how we perceive risk, sometimes forgetting to consider the client's viewpoint. The industry has trained us to start client relationships with a risk assessment questionnaire. You know the one: "On a scale of 1 to 10, how comfortable are you with market volatility?"

These assessments aim to quantify a client's emotional risk tolerance. But here's the catch: emotions are fickle. They're influenced by everything from last night's sleep to this morning's news headline. How someone feels about risk on a sunny day after a hearty breakfast might be entirely different from how they feel on a rainy Monday before coffee.

Basing long-term financial strategies on such volatile sentiments is like building a house of cards in a wind tunnel. Sure, it might stand for a moment, but it won't withstand the slightest gust.

THE INDUSTRY'S SAFETY NET—OR IS IT?

Let's be honest: these risk assessments often serve more to protect us as financial advisors and our firms than to benefit clients. They're a compliance checkbox, a way to cover our bases if things go south. It's like asking Lisa how scared she is before entering the haunted house but then doing nothing to adjust the experience for her while she is walking through it.

The financial industry's reliance on rules of thumb, like the "Rule of 100"—subtracting a client's age from 100 to determine the percentage of their portfolio that should be in stocks—is another example of this one-size-fits-all mentality. But consider Warren Buffett, who in his nineties remained heavily invested in stocks. He famously said, "Diversification is protection against ignorance. It makes little sense if you know what you are doing."

Maybe you're thinking, "Yeah, but that's Warren Buffett. Our clients aren't as smart as he is. They could never afford that type of risk." If you think that way, remember that Buffett is investing on behalf of his clients—just like you are on behalf of yours.

Target-date funds are yet another way the industry tries to automate risk management. They adjust asset allocation based on a target retirement date, effectively putting the investment strategy on autopilot. It's convenient but impersonal, like getting on a roller coaster that's the same for everyone regardless of whether you're a thrill seeker or prefer the teacups. Don't even get me started on how horrible their performance has been compared to simple benchmark portfolios.

THE PROBLEM WITH EMOTIONAL RISK

Emotional risk is all about how clients *feel* about volatility. And while feelings are important, they're not the most reliable foundation for a financial plan. Clients might say they can't stomach a 20 percent drop in their portfolio, but if their income needs are met, does that drop affect their day-to-day life?

During the market downturn at the onset of the COVID-19 pandemic, I overheard a conversation between two young employees at a grocery store. One said to the other, "I'm done losing money. I cashed out my 401(k)." His emotional reaction to market volatility led him to make a decision that, in hindsight, likely cost him significant future gains.

Emotions can rob clients of rational decision-making. They see their account balances dip and panic, much like Lisa panicking at every creak and shadow in the haunted house, even though she was never in any real danger.

DEVELOPING A PERSONALIZED RISK PHILOSOPHY

Recognizing the limitations of traditional risk assessments, advisors must develop their risk philosophy—one that aligns with both their professional expertise and their clients' unique needs, as well as the planning software they use. This personalized approach goes beyond generic questionnaires and dives deep into understanding the client's life goals, financial necessities, and emotional comfort with risk.

THE IMPORTANCE OF A TAILORED APPROACH

Every client is different, and so is their perception of risk. Just as Lisa and I had contrasting experiences in the haunted house, clients have varying comfort levels with financial uncertainty. A one-size-fits-all strategy doesn't serve anyone well. Advisors should strive to create a risk philosophy that:

- Aligns with the client's financial goals and income needs
- Respects the client's emotional tolerance for market fluctuations
- Adapts to changing life circumstances and market conditions

OUR PHILOSOPHY: BALANCING MINDSETS AND NEEDS

In our practice, we've developed a risk philosophy that's integrated into our planning approach—Simplicitree, which I've written about throughout. This philosophy recognizes that clients generally fall into one of several mindsets regarding risk and financial goals. By identifying these mindsets, we tailor our investment strategies to align with what truly matters to each client.

We have three mindsets for risk management:

- Retirement Risk Tolerance
- Preservation Risk Tolerance
- Legacy Risk Tolerance

For some clients, the focus is on maximizing retirement income without concern for leaving a financial legacy. They're comfortable spending down their assets to enjoy their retirement fully. Others aim to preserve their wealth while still enjoying a comfortable lifestyle, focusing on generating predictable income and accepting market fluctuations as a manageable risk. Then some prioritize building a legacy for future generations, willing to accept greater risk for the potential of long-term growth.

By understanding which mindset resonates with a client, we can balance their need for income with their emotional comfort regarding risk. This approach allows us to craft investment strategies that not only meet financial objectives but also provide peace of mind.

ANCHORING CLIENTS WITH NEEDS-BASED PLANNING

Years ago, I got into a conversation with a head compliance officer for one of the big three financial institutions. I asked him a very direct question. "If your model for risk tolerance forces you to recommend a portfolio that is safe but almost certainly will not provide the income the client needs throughout retirement, what will you do?" He paused for a moment, asked a few qualifying questions, and responded with "Well, we would be forced to recommend a solution that fits their risk profile and place their income needs in the back seat."

I pushed a little more. "Do you mean to tell me that you would recommend a solution that would run a client out of money just to make sure you checked the risk tolerance box?" He said, unfortunately, yes—we have to. It would never be our intention to run a client out of money, but we are forced to put risk first above all else.

This is my opinion: that's stupid. Who is that rule protecting? The client or the advisor?

Let me change this question slightly for you, but be honest in your response. So, what's more important: wanting to avoid discomfort from market swings or needing to secure a reliable income for your client? Be honest when you answer.

When we focus on clients' actual needs—like paying bills, funding retirement, or leaving a legacy—we anchor their financial plans to tangible goals rather than fleeting emotions. If you base your risk tolerance rules on feelings and wants, then you would be protecting yourself. If you base your risk tolerance on what a client needs for retirement income, then you would be protecting your client. I am not sure why the industry has this wrong; it seems pretty cut and dry to me.

THE REAL PRIORITY: INCOME OVER VOLATILITY

You can't spend volatility. Clients can't pay their mortgage with a low standard deviation. What they need is income. By shifting the focus from managing emotional reactions to securing income streams, we provide clients with something tangible and reliable. Let me share a story that drove this point home for me.

A TALE OF TWO CRISES

A few years ago, a client came to my office looking particularly distressed. As they sat down in my office, it was very clear that something was wrong. I cut straight to the point: "What's going on? You seem very distressed." He then shared that in the same week, his wife had been diagnosed with cancer and he had lost his job. Talk about a haunted house of horrors.

We had previously structured their portfolio to generate steady dividend income, aligned with their specific financial mindset and goals, and now all we had to do was turn on that income to help reduce some of their financial anxiety.

About a year later, I wanted to check back in with them and see how things were going and revisit their income plan. As I revisited their plan, I was anxious about how market volatility might be affecting them, especially given their personal challenges and because the market had gone into a downward spiral.

When they came in for a review during a particularly volatile market period, I discussed the recent fluctuations. The husband stopped me mid-sentence.

"Do you think we are worried about market volatility?" he asked.

"Well, given everything that's happening, I thought you might be," I replied.

He leaned forward and said, "The dividend income from our portfolio has been our lifeline. We're not concerned about the market ups and downs. We're concerned about paying our bills, and you've helped us do that." He went on to say, "That dividend income saved our lives."

That moment was a revelation. It underscored the importance of focusing on clients' needs rather than their fluctuating emotional responses to the market. It also reiterated that when a client takes ownership of their plan and its income strategy, that changes everything! Fluctuations in the market don't have the same impact as they did before I helped clients take ownership of their income solutions.

LOGICAL PLANNING OVER EMOTIONAL GUESSWORK

By prioritizing needs-based planning and integrating a personalized risk philosophy, we help clients build a financial fortress that's less susceptible to the whims of the market—and their emotions.

THE ADVISOR'S ROLE: FROM PROTECTOR TO EMPOWERER

When we focus on meeting clients' income needs and align our strategies with their risk mindsets, we become more than just financial advisors; we become partners in their journey. We're not just protecting ourselves with compliance checklists; we're empowering clients to take ownership of their financial futures.

This approach also changes the dynamic when the market takes a downturn. Instead of panicked calls from clients wanting to jump ship, we get fewer calls because clients understand their income needs are still being met. They have an anchor point—a reliable income stream—that keeps them grounded when everything else seems uncertain.

THE REFERRAL EFFECT

When clients feel secure and empowered, they're more likely to refer friends and family, not because we've asked them to, but because they genuinely believe in the value we're providing.

In the past, I invested heavily in referral programs—fancy dinners, elaborate rewards, you name it. The results were good, but at a cost of marketing, which lowered the impact of the referral. But since shifting the focus to needs-based planning and embracing our risk philosophy, referrals have increased organically without any marketing cost or even the need to ask for one. Clients appreciate the peace of mind we've provided and are eager to share that with others. When you believe in something and when that something changes your life, you want to share it with everyone you care about. This is why ownership is so important.

JUSTIFYING RECOMMENDATIONS WITH CONFIDENCE

From a compliance standpoint, basing recommendations on clients' needs and clearly defined risk philosophies makes our advice more defensible. If problems were to come up, we could demonstrate that our recommendations were based on concrete needs and long-term goals, aligned with their personal risk mindset—not on how they happened to feel on a particular Tuesday afternoon.

Even more, our risk philosophy is connected so deeply into our planning process of Simplicitree that clients not only understand it, but they want it. Again, I can't say this enough. When a client takes ownership of their income plan and the risk that comes along with it, they are comfortable with any struggles ahead. If changes are required, then you can make them together.

GUIDING CLIENTS THROUGH HAUNTED HOUSES

Risk is subjective and multifaceted. Like a haunted house, it can be thrilling or terrifying, depending on one's perspective. As advisors, our job isn't to eliminate the haunted house but to guide our clients through it safely.

By developing and adhering to a personalized risk philosophy and focusing on needs-based planning, we help clients navigate the twists and turns without being paralyzed by every shadow or eerie sound. We provide them with an anchor, a steady hand in the dark, so they can move forward with confidence.

In doing so, we not only protect our clients but also build stronger, more trusting relationships. We shift from being just another face in the financial industry to becoming an indispensable partner in our clients' lives.

So the next time you're tempted to rely solely on a risk tolerance questionnaire, remember Lisa in the haunted house. Ask yourself: Are you addressing your client's real fears and needs, or are you just handing them a flashlight with dead batteries?

Every advisor should consider developing their risk philosophy— one that respects the unique needs and mindsets of their clients. By doing so, we can focus on what truly matters: empowering our clients to achieve their dreams regardless of the market's haunted halls.

Part 3

YOUR CO-PLANNING DEEP DIVE

CHAPTER 9

WILDERNESS AND WEALTH MANAGEMENT

*Stop Presenting and Start Co-Planning
Alongside the Client*

At heart, I'm a bona fide city slicker and wannabe beach bum. Give me skyscrapers and sandy beaches over sequoias any day of the week. I love technology, my daily habits and routines, and the convenience of having everything I need at the push of a button. Why rough it when you can smooth it, right?

When I was newly married and my church invited me to a "wild" retreat in Algonquin Provincial Park, Canada—somewhere so far north it's practically hugging Santa Claus—I thought, "I'm up for the challenge. I mean, it's just camping. How wild could a *wild* retreat really get?"

The retreat leaders looked like they bench-pressed grizzly bears and flossed with pine needles. When they gave us a rundown of what to pack, they said, "Pack light; pack smart; pack only what you need." I went home, watched some YouTube videos titled "Camping Hacks for Dummies," and did a little online research (i.e., I Googled "camping gadgets"). I brought some of the gear they suggested, but I also packed my electric razor…a guy has to maintain some standards.

Fast-forward to the retreat. We're in the middle of nowhere, surrounded by trees taller than my apartment building. The mosquitoes were the size of hummingbirds; bug spray tasted like dessert to them.

When our guides told us to grab our backpacks, they said, "Everything you need for the next week should be in there." Food, shelter, clothing, survival gear—you name it. Did I mention the canoe? Yeah, we also had to carry a canoe. Our task for the week? To paddle all day, portage over mountains with our gear and canoe, and repeat. Every. Single. Day. It was like *Groundhog Day* meets *Survivor*.

On day one, I felt confident. Paddling with my partner, soaking in the serene beauty, I thought, "I've got this wilderness thing down. Maybe I'll start a vlog." Then we hit our first portage. Let me paint a picture: there I was with my overpacked backpack—fifty-five pounds in all, including my electric razor and AA batteries—struggling to lift the sixty-five-pound canoe over my head, all while trudging up a mountain that seemed like Mount Everest's Canadian cousin. Halfway up that mountain, I realized I'd made a huge mistake. My city-boy research didn't prepare me for this. Every step was a revelation. Some things you just can't learn on YouTube!

By day three, I was a broken man. My razor remained untouched in my pack, mocking me every morning as I struggled to pack up with hands that felt like lead. My shoulders ached from carrying the canoe, my legs were jelly, and my carefully curated *necessities* were extra weight. I would have traded all my batteries for a decent night's sleep on something that wasn't a rock.

Reality had slapped me in the face with a pine branch. Everything I'd read online, every video I'd watched, every bit of research I had done paled in comparison to the real deal. The wilderness is a great teacher; I was learning the hard way.

Somewhere between wringing out my socks and swatting away a mosquito, it all hit me: you can look at pictures, read books, and watch videos all day long, but nothing beats the power of firsthand experience.

And yes, this lesson applies to financial planning. As advisors, we can read reports, look at charts, and listen to experts, but until we see the impact of our decisions in real time, it's all just theory. And if this is true for you as a financial advisor, imagine how much harder this is for investors.

OUT OF THE WILD: THE POWER OF CO-PLANNING

Many financial advisors think they can plan effectively without involving their clients in the process. Presenting solutions to a client is completely different from co-planning with them. In the same way I needed to experience the wilderness firsthand to understand it, clients need to be involved in their financial planning to grasp the full picture.

When we work with clients using our Simplicitree software, we don't just present a plan. We co-plan alongside them. We let them see exactly what we see. They can test different strategies, see the real impact of moving money here or there, and understand how one decision can completely change their financial future. It's like putting them in the driver's seat of their financial canoe, letting them experience every portage and paddle stroke without the blisters.

Let me take you through how this works.

TURNING RED PROBLEMS INTO GREEN SOLUTIONS

We've just finished going through the base plan with a client, really digging into the shortfall. Now it's time to discuss investment strategies—a whole section of Simplicitree where we get to solve the shortfall in real time.

When we first bring up the investment planning tab in Simplicitree, it looks like a blank canvas—gray boxes everywhere. This isn't a glitch; it's by design. We want to start a conversation with our client about what they asked us to do. Typically, at the end of the base plan, when we're talking about their shortfall, there's a sea of red numbers glaring back at them like the eyes of that mocking mosquito. Once we get them to ask the question "What would you do?" the magic happens. The transition of ownership begins.

We strategize in the moment with them. We might say, "Okay, let's consider moving this old 401(k) into an IRA." Once that happens, we then apply investment strategies to the investment. We might begin with an annuity, then change to a mutual fund or switch to bonds. With each strategy, their plan instantly changes. Here's the real magic: the client is involved. Hands on the keyboard, they're clicking buttons and seeing the immediate impact of these moves.

Instead of asking, "Why are you recommending this investment?" they ask, "Why wouldn't I invest in this strategy?" Or they're saying, "That doesn't look good. Is there something better?"

This is the same process many advisors follow when they're in between meetings. They look at one investment strategy after another to find the right selections to create a plan worth investing in. The biggest difference between that and what I wrote above is this: we invite clients into the process. Doing so can change everything for your practice.

THE PSYCHOLOGY BEHIND THIS

By involving clients directly, we're making it real for them. It's no longer hypothetical. They're taking action and seeing the consequences (good and bad) of their choices in real time. By highlighting their problem, we also actively work with them to solve it. Plus, we've severed any emotional attachment to previous investments.

Clients will sit there with anticipation building, waiting for us to explain how to fix their shortfall. It's like they're at the bottom of a mountain, looking up, struggling with their canoe, asking, "How are we going to get over this?" Then we begin the climb.

GAMIFYING FINANCIAL PLANNING

One of the features of Simplicitree is our pill chart: a visual representation of their shortfall. It starts at zero, a red empty pill. Our goal is to fill it up to 100 percent, turning it green. We've essentially gamified the process.

As we add different investment strategies—annuities, bonds, CDs, mutual funds, dividends, you name it—the client sees how each decision fills up the pill. It's immediate feedback.

We might add one strategy that is heavy on mutual funds, and the pill chart goes from 0 to 54 percent, or maybe 63 percent. This is a great moment. We haven't solved anything yet, but now the investor sees what's going on. They understand that as we add investments or strategies, we're moving toward solving their shortfall.

As we continue, the client sees the impact on their projected income. It's like we're helping them try on different backpacks before their hike—some are too heavy, some don't fit right, but eventually, we'll find one that suits them perfectly. And the whole time, the client is immersed, learning, and taking it to heart.

Sidenote here: there are times when no matter how hard you try, or how many solutions you add, you just can't make it work. These moments are okay. Here's why: when you co-plan, clients see their problems and understand when they need to lower expectations. You don't have to be the bad guy or the bearer of bad news. Just let them see what you see.

OWNERSHIP THROUGH INVOLVEMENT

I've been hitting the ownership bell since at least Chapter 6. Let me restate my key point: when we involve clients, they take ownership of the solution. It's no longer *us* telling *them* what to do. Instead, *we're* working together to find the best path forward. This is how I should have approached my camping trip—not by assuming I knew better, but by engaging with the experienced guides and learning from them.

In traditional financial planning, advisors often present a sixty-page report filled with charts and graphs that might as well be in another language. Clients nod, perhaps too embarrassed to admit they don't understand. With co-planning, the process is transparent. Clients see the immediate effects of different strategies and understand why certain investment strategies work, while others don't.

RISK REIMAGINED

In my wilderness story, I underestimated the risk because I didn't truly understand it. Similarly, the financial industry often approaches risk in a way that's, dare I say, misguided. Advisors lead with risk assessments, confining clients to predetermined boxes. But risk is subjective. There's the risk of running out of money and the risk of temporary fluctuations in account value. Which is more critical to the client?

When we co-plan, we don't start by pigeonholing clients into a risk category. Instead, we explore different strategies together, showing them how each affects their income and long-term goals. Only then do we have an informed discussion about acceptable risk. It's like deciding whether to pack that electric razor—you might think it's necessary, but once you're halfway up a mountain, you realize what's truly important.

BEYOND THE MONTE CARLO

Many advisors rely on Monte Carlo simulations that might show a 70 percent chance of success. But what about the other 30 percent? Would you get on a plane that had a 30 percent chance of crashing? I wouldn't.

With co-planning, we aim for strategies that fill that pill chart to 100 percent and also provide a significant margin for error. We're doing more than *hoping* things work out. We're planning for success even when the unexpected happens.

This type of education is empowering. Let me explain. During market downturns, our clients haven't panicked. Why? Because they understood their strategies. They knew how their investments worked and why they were the ones we chose. Some clients even called to ask if they could invest more. That's the power of education and involvement.

Remember those annual reviews I talked about in Chapter 5? We show clients the strength of their portfolios even during market downturns. We've gone through the 2008 financial crisis, the dot-com bubble, and the 2020 pandemic. In all cases, we've had more income at the end of the year than we started with. That has a lot to do with knowing the resilience of good dividend strategies.

The long and short of it: when clients understand their investments, they're less likely to make fear-based decisions. They're confident because they've been part of the planning process. Just like I would have been better prepared for the wilderness if I had taken the time to learn from those who knew it best, clients are better prepared for financial storms when they're educated and involved.

THE COMPLIANCE COMFORT

From a compliance standpoint, co-planning is effective and prudent. We've been audited multiple times and have passed with flying colors each time. One auditor even mentioned she wished more advisors used this type of solution because of the transparency and client involvement it fosters. Another auditor pulled me aside and said, "I'm not allowed to recommend financial planning software, but if I could, Simplicitree would be the only one I would recommend."

That unofficial recommendation goes a long way in helping us believe in our co-planning process.

THE CO-PLANNING ADVANTAGE

The next time someone tells you to "pack light" in life or finances, take their advice. It doesn't matter whether you're in the wild or planning someone's financial future. There's no substitute for firsthand experience—because no one remembers the slideshow, but everyone remembers the hike.

Presenting solutions to a client is completely different from co-planning with them. By engaging clients in the planning process, you empower them to understand, take ownership, and make informed decisions that align with their goals.

CHAPTER 10

THE LOOK

Transform Red Fears to an
Empowered Green Reality

Even though I am not a natural-born camper, I enjoy it and went back for more torture for four years straight. On my last camping trip to Algonquin Provincial Park—older and wiser with slightly less of a death wish—I figured I'd upgrade my canoe situation. Rather than lugging a sixty-five-pound model, I teamed up with one of the leaders who brought along a thirty-pound carbon fiber canoe. Even with its paddle, it was so light I thought it might float away if I let go. Everything was easier, faster, and smoother, like trading in a clunker for a sports car. We'd often start at the back of the pack, just for kicks, and by the time we reached the first portage, we'd be leading the charge, high-fiving each other like we'd just discovered fire.

Halfway through the trip, he threw a curveball. "I want to switch partners," he said. Before I could protest, he paired me with Out-of-Shape Oliver. Oliver had never seen a canoe up close, let alone paddled one. My new canoe felt like it was made of lead, and its paddles could have doubled as medieval weapons.

Portaging, a fancy term for "let's carry this heavy thing over a mountain," is usually a team effort. You carry the canoe for a bit, then your partner takes over, and so on. But Oliver could barely manage twenty-five steps before gasping, "I can't do this anymore!" I became the human mule for the rest of the trip.

By day two, I was a cocktail of frustration and muscle cramps. We'd start near the front, but by the first portage, we were so far behind, I half-expected to find dinosaur fossils. All the while, I silently plotted ways to make Oliver "accidentally" fall into the lake.

On day three, it started raining—not a gentle drizzle, but a full-on monsoon, the kind of rain where the drops are so big they create their own splashback. Sitting in the middle of this lake, I seethed behind Oliver, who was blissfully unaware, probably contemplating what flavor of ice cream he wanted.

Then, amid this downpour, he turned around with the biggest grin I'd ever seen. "Isn't God's beauty incredible?" he exclaimed. "Look at that eagle soaring above us! We're in the middle of paradise! Sure, we're getting rained on, but we're also being showered with nature's glory!"

I was speechless. Here I was, fixated on my misery, while Oliver was soaking in—literally and figuratively—the beauty around us. It hit me like a ton of wet canoes: I needed to get over myself and see things from a different perspective.

BUILDING THE PLAN TOGETHER

As financial planners, we often get caught up in our processes and frustrations. We forget to see things from our clients' points of view. They come to us in all sorts of emotional states—anxious, excited, and overwhelmed. We need to step outside of ourselves and truly engage with where they are. Ultimately, it's not about us. It's about guiding them on their journey.

In our practice, our co-planning process embodies this shift in perspective. We don't dictate terms; we involve them in every step, making them active participants in their financial journey.

To review, we begin this process by creating what we call the "base plan." This is essentially stripping out all strategies and investments to see what their financial shortfall is. It's like showing them a map of their financial landscape without any filters—just the raw, unvarnished truth. And yes, sometimes that means a lot of red ink.

I remember one client who, upon seeing their base plan, looked like he'd just bitten into a lemon. "Is that…all red?" he asked.

"I'm afraid so," I replied. "But don't worry, we're here to find a solution together."

CRAFTING THE INVESTMENT STRATEGY

Next, we look into investment strategies like we went over in the last chapter. We help the client understand the realities of different approaches, the risks involved, and how each strategy aligns with their goals and temperament. This isn't about dazzling them with jargon or overwhelming them with charts; it's about education.

During this phase, we often see clients move from a place of anxiety to a sense of clarity and control. They're not just hearing about solutions—we're showing them *why* those solutions work, how they align with their values, and what tradeoffs come with each path. Their involvement transforms the experience: instead of being sold an investment strategy, they're equipped to choose one—because it makes sense, not because it was delivered with a polished pitch.

UNVEILING THE INCOME PLAN

Now comes the exciting part: unveiling the income plan. This is the result of all the strategy and planning—a tangible, visual representation of their financial future. And the transformation from the base plan is often dramatic.

Remember all that red ink on the base plan? Well, after you find the right income solution to solve their shortfall, all of their red turns green. And let me tell you, green is a much more comfortable color. It's like the difference between a stop sign and a green light—one tells you to halt, the other says, "Go ahead; you're clear."

I had a client once who, upon seeing the income plan, broke into the biggest smile. "Wait, where did all the red go?" she asked.

"It's gone," I said. "Because we've solved your shortfall together."

But it's crucial to remind them this plan isn't magic. It requires action. "This is your plan," I tell them. "But it only becomes reality if you decide to implement it."

The process of Simplicitree is simple, and there will be a glaring difference between how you plan with them and what they get from other financial advisors. When you help a client understand their shortfall and then solve it alongside them—and the drumroll please—unveiling their income plan is simply magical. If you allow me to beat a dead horse, this process is how clients take ownership of their plan and the strategy that makes it work.

THE PSYCHOLOGY AT PLAY

What's fascinating is the psychology at play during this process. Clients often feel a sense of pride and relief when they see the income plan. They helped create it; they took ownership. It's not something that was handed down to them; they helped build it; they understand it and believe in the investment strategy that solved their shortfall.

But there's also an important dynamic here: by involving them in the process, we're reinforcing their decisions at every step. They're less likely to get cold feet because they've been active participants, not just passive observers.

LANGUAGE MATTERS: IT'S THEIR PLAN

One thing we've learned is the importance of language. We make sure to refer to it as "your plan," "your solution," "your income." This isn't about us; it's about them. And by using this language, we reinforce their ownership and involvement.

I recall a moment when a client leaned back in his chair and said, "This is my plan, isn't it?"

"Absolutely," I replied. "You built it, and it's all yours."

Some of our advisors often refer to this as "the look." That moment when the light bulb goes off inside a client's mind, where they truly understand their plan and take ownership of it. As a teacher, not a financial advisor, this look lets me know they got it. This business is amazing!

ADDRESSING CONCERNS WITH SURPLUS

Another powerful aspect of the income plan is the concept of surplus. This isn't just about meeting their income needs; it's about having excess—margin for error, if you will.

Clients often worry about things like long-term care costs, unexpected expenses, or leaving a legacy for their heirs. By showing them the surplus in their plan, we can address these concerns directly.

For instance, if they have an $80,000 surplus each year and are worried about potential long-term care costs, we can show them that they already have a built-in buffer. It's like having an umbrella before it starts to rain.

THE EPIPHANY: NO ASSUMED GROWTH NEEDED

One of the most enlightening moments for clients is when they realize the plan doesn't assume any growth in their investments—only the income from dividends or other investment-income strategies.

"Wait," they'll say, "you're not assuming any rate of return?"

"Nope," I reply. "We're basing this entire plan on the historical yields of your dividend-paying investments moving forward."

"So what happens if it does grow?" they'll ask, eyes widening.

"Well, that's just icing on the cake," I tell them.

This shifts the risk conversation entirely. Instead of hoping for market growth to meet their needs, they see that their plan is sustainable even without it. It provides a level of security and peace of mind that's hard to overstate.

CHANGING THE NARRATIVE AROUND RISK

This approach changes how clients perceive risk. They're no longer fixated on chasing returns or worried about market volatility. Instead, they understand their income needs are met through reliable dividend income, not speculative growth.

I often joke that we're not trying to be **rock stars on growth**; we're focusing on being **rock solid on income**. And the irony is, when you stop trying to be a rock star on growth, you often end up performing better in the long run.

THE RIPPLE EFFECT: CLIENTS BECOME ADVOCATES

The impact of this process goes beyond the individual client. Because they've been so involved and empowered, they often become enthusiastic advocates.

I had a client who was so taken with the process that she asked if she could bring in her son. "He's just out of college," she said. "He doesn't have much money yet, but I want him to get started on the right foot."

Her son came in, and we spent a few meetings setting him up with a simple dividend strategy that he could manage on his own. He wasn't in a position to become a client then, but that didn't matter.

Over the years, he's referred nearly twenty people to us—some of whom have become very large clients.

Similarly, an advisor in our firm shared a story about a client who kept referring friends and family after going through the process. "I don't even ask for referrals," he said. "They just keep coming, and I keep asking, how many people does this guy know?"

THE ADVISOR'S PERSPECTIVE: LESS PRESSURE, MORE FULFILLMENT

As advisors, this process also changes our experience. There are no high-pressure sales tactics, no sweaty palms, hoping a client will sign on the dotted line. Instead, we guide them through a journey of discovery and empowerment.

One advisor mentioned that before using this approach, he never got referrals. Now he can't stop them from coming in. Another pointed out how client conversations have changed. Clients will want to update their plan when considering a major purchase or life change. "Can we see how this affects my plan?" they'll ask.

It's a shift from us being the gatekeepers of financial wisdom to being guides who empower clients to make informed financial decisions. And it's incredibly rewarding.

INVOLVING CLIENTS: THE KEY TO LEARNING AND GROWTH

It all comes back to perspective and involvement. Benjamin Franklin is credited with saying, "Tell me and I'll forget. Teach me and I may remember. Involve me and I learn."

By involving clients in the planning process, we help them learn and take ownership. They become the heroes of their own financial stories, and we're the guides helping them along the way.

I often notice that during meetings, clients get so engaged that they stand next to me, pointing at the touch screen on my wall, asking questions, and making suggestions. They're not just involved; they're taking control. It's a joy to see that level of engagement.

STEPPING OUTSIDE OURSELVES

Just like I needed to step outside of my frustration on that canoe trip and see the beauty around me, we as financial advisors need to step outside of ourselves and truly engage with our clients' perspectives. By involving them, educating them, and empowering them, we create not just clients but advocates—people who are excited about their financial futures and eager to share that excitement with others.

So let's put down our heavy canoes and clunky paddles, and pick up the tools that make the journey smoother—not just for us, but for the clients we serve.

CHAPTER 11

WAX ON, WAX OFF

Teach Finance Through Familiar Connections

There once was a young man who was uprooted to a new place. He struggled to find his footing both socially and physically. Seeking guidance, he turned to an unassuming mentor—a quiet handyman with a knack for fixing things and a passion for trimming small trees. Instead of straightforward lessons, the mentor handed him a sponge and a bucket of soapy water.

"Wash the car," he said.

Perplexed but eager to learn, the young man spent days washing cars, painting fences, and sanding floors. Frustration mounted as he failed to see how these mundane chores related to his goal. Just when he was about to throw in the towel—quite literally—the mentor revealed the hidden wisdom behind the tasks. Each movement had been secretly training him, building muscle memory and discipline.

Suddenly, everything clicked. The young man's eyes widened as he realized he'd been learning all along, just not in the way he'd expected. Does this story sound familiar?

If you guessed the original *The Karate Kid*, then you guessed right.

Mr. Miyagi taught Daniel-san essential karate techniques through simple chores. Daniel's frustration mirrored the experience of many who seek to learn but feel overwhelmed by traditional methods. Mr. Miyagi's genius played out by associating the unfamiliar with the familiar, making the difficult seem almost instinctive.

In my practice, I once witnessed a client's "Daniel-san moment" purely by accident. Midway through explaining a dense financial concept, I realized he was thoroughly confused. Instead of pressing on, I asked about his job, and he mentioned running a small contracting business. Suddenly, I saw a way to connect the principle he found so confusing—future dividend distribution projections—with the basics of estimating labor and materials for a construction project. In that moment, I watched his eyes light up as everything clicked, just like Daniel when he finally understood "wax on, wax off."

The instant he saw the parallel between his work and my financial advice, I had my realization: this was exactly how I could help clients and prospects fully grasp the planning process. In the coming pages, I'm going to share the very techniques that helped me create that flash of insight so you, too, can give all your clients and prospects their own Daniel-san moments—effortlessly turning confusion into clarity and frustration into understanding.

In your practice as a financial advisor, you can apply the same principle. When trying to teach clients or colleagues complex financial concepts, start with something they already know well. Draw parallels between their daily experiences and the financial strategies you want them to understand. Whether it's likening investment diversification to a balanced diet or explaining market volatility through the ups and downs of their favorite sports team's season, education by association can transform confusion into clarity and hesitation into confidence.

Just like the young apprentice, they'll soon learn that seemingly mundane aspects of their lives are tools that unlock profound financial understanding.

MAKING THE COMPLEX UNDERSTANDABLE

Our clients come to us navigating a complex and often confusing financial landscape. Even concepts that seem straightforward to us—like dividends, which have been around for centuries—can feel like advanced calculus to them. Even worse, it could be something they think they know, but what they believe is actually wrong.

Consider this: when you buy a pack of gum, how much research do you do? Probably none. It's a low-stakes decision. But when purchasing a new TV, you might compare models, read reviews, and perhaps even measure your living room wall twice. Upgrade that decision to buying a car or a house and the research intensifies exponentially.

Now imagine making decisions about your entire life savings—the nest egg that needs to last through retirement. The gravity of understanding every nuance becomes paramount. Yet many clients feel overwhelmed by the sheer complexity of financial planning.

INTRODUCING EDUCATION BY ASSOCIATION

This is where the concept of education by association comes into play. It's a teaching technique that connects new, complex information to something the client already understands deeply.

The idea sprouted during a study group session years ago. I was explaining a financial concept when one of the advisors in the room interrupted, visibly puzzled.

"What made you think of that?" he asked.

At first, I didn't understand what he was asking because, to me, the connection was obvious. When I encounter something unfamiliar, my brain instinctively tries to link it to something I already know to make a connection. It's like using a map of a city you've visited to navigate a new one—different streets, but similar layouts.

This approach isn't new; it's how we're taught from the earliest grades. Each year's curriculum builds upon the last, adding layers to our foundational knowledge. Why should financial education be any different?

CONNECTING DOTS WITH CABLES AND CORDS

Remember the old days of connecting a VCR to a TV? You had those red, white, and yellow cables—each serving a specific function. Video and two audio channels, if memory serves.

Fast-forward to today, and we have HDMI cables—a single cord that handles everything. For someone baffled by technology, explaining HDMI as the modern equivalent of those three old cables can make the new seem familiar.

I use this same strategy when explaining financial concepts. If a client understands real estate, I might compare dividends to rental income. If they're tech-savvy, I might liken market volatility to software updates—sometimes beneficial, sometimes disruptive, but always part of the process.

STORIES FROM THE FIELD

I once met an investor who was, let's say, exceptionally confident. He was selling his veterinary practice and believed he had everything figured out. "I'm good," he declared, with a wave of his hand that suggested our meeting was merely a formality. He didn't need any help, especially mine.

Intrigued, I dug deeper. He was keeping the building where his practice was housed and had secured a twenty-year lease with the new owners. He didn't care about the property's fluctuating value because he had consistent rental income—much like dividends.

I pointed this out. "You know," I said, "your building is like a dividend-paying stock. The value might go up or down, but you're receiving predictable and consistent income regardless."

His eyes widened. "I never thought of it that way."

At that moment, the light bulb switched on. The conversation shifted from him wanting to leave as quickly as possible to an engaging discussion about income strategies and financial planning.

Another time, I spoke with a woman who owned farmland. She rented it out annually to a farmer, receiving a fixed amount per acre regardless of the crop's success. When I compared her rental income to dividends—a steady income irrespective of market conditions—she grasped the concept immediately.

"It's like I'm getting paid just for owning the land," she mused.

"Exactly," I replied. "Just like dividends pay you for owning shares."

THE POWER OF QUESTIONS

This technique isn't a one-size-fits-all solution. Sometimes, despite my best efforts, I can't find an immediate association. It's like trying to explain the taste of an apple to someone who's only ever eaten oranges.

That's when I start asking more questions. What do they do for a living? What hobbies do they enjoy? What's something they're passionate about? The more I learn, the better chance I have of finding that perfect analogy.

One client was an engineer fascinated by bridges. I compared his investment strategy to bridge design, emphasizing the importance of many dividend-paying stocks that would represent the bridge's structural support. His face lit up.

"So, if one support weakens, the bridge doesn't collapse?"

"Exactly," I said. "Diversification strengthens your financial bridge."

SHIFTING FOCUS FROM SELLING TO TEACHING

Here's the thing: our industry often emphasizes closing the deal. Techniques are honed to nudge clients toward a yes. But I've found when clients truly understand their financial plans, the need for persuasive tactics diminishes.

It's like our young friend Daniel-san finally grasping the purpose behind waxing cars and painting fences. Once he understood the *why*, his commitment to the process—and Mr. Miyagi—increased tenfold.

By focusing on education, we empower our clients. They move from passive participants to active decision-makers in their financial journeys. They take ownership, and with that comes confidence and trust.

Here's the crazy part: when you truly teach a concept they fully grasp, they never want to let you go. Just like in *The Karate Kid*, Daniel-san always went back to Mr. Miyagi for advice and guidance. He never got to a place where he didn't need him, and that's exactly how this works. The more you teach, the more you give away, the more clients want you in their lives.

EMBRACING YOUR INNER MR. MIYAGI

Channeling your inner mentor—be it a quiet handyman with a knack for karate or a dedicated advisor—requires patience and practice. It's not always easy. There will be times when you feel like you're speaking a different language.

But when that moment of clarity arrives, it's incredibly rewarding. Seeing a client's eyes light up with understanding is one of the greatest joys in our profession. It's the equivalent of watching someone ride a bike without training wheels for the first time.

And yes, sometimes you'll need a sense of humor. Not every analogy will land perfectly. I once tried to explain market liquidity to a client by comparing it to ketchup flowing out of a bottle. Let's just say that one didn't stick, but it did illustrate why financial advising is considered a practice. We won't always get it right or find perfection, but we always have to keep trying to move forward. I believe the best way I can serve clients is to teach them what I know, just like I'm teaching you. If you truly want to grow your practice, stop selling and start educating—the real kind of education, like Mr. Miyagi made famous.

THE LONG GAME

Mastering education by association isn't an overnight process. It takes time to develop the skill of making complex concepts relatable. But with each conversation, you'll get better. You'll see patterns and make connections more quickly.

Remember, our goal isn't just to manage assets; it's to build relationships founded on trust and understanding. When clients feel educated and empowered, they're more likely to stick around for the long haul—and most importantly, they will refer others.

Just as Daniel-san learned martial arts through everyday chores, our clients can master their financial futures when we present information in a way that resonates with them.

The next time you're sitting across from a client who looks as confused as someone trying to assemble furniture with instructions in Swedish, take a step back. Ask questions. Find that common ground. Connect the unfamiliar to the familiar.

Who knows? You might just help them "wax on, wax off" their way to financial enlightenment.

Remember, as a wise mentor once said, "Before you can run, you must first learn to walk." In our case, first learn to understand, then learn to invest.

PRACTICE MAKES PROFICIENT

Don't be discouraged if it doesn't click right away. Like any art, education by association improves with practice. Engage with colleagues, role-play scenarios, and don't hesitate to reflect on your experiences. This is why we do so many study groups with our advisors. If you ever stop learning, you are done.

I've had moments where I thought a client understood everything, only to find out later they were as lost as ever. It's humbling but also a reminder that teaching is a journey, not a destination.

Stay dedicated, keep refining your approach, and soon enough, making these connections will become second nature. Your clients will thank you, and your practice will flourish. After all, empowering others through education isn't just beneficial—it's the most rewarding part of what we do.

Speaking of practice, let's stay on that topic for a bit.

CHAPTER 12

ALL-IN EXCELLENCE

Greatness Demands All-In Excellence

It was the summer of 1995, and Michael Jordan found himself in an unfamiliar position: on the losing side. I remember because I was watching, along with most of America and probably two-thirds of the world. Even though the scene felt surreal, I couldn't tear my eyes away. Part of me wondered if we were witnessing the twilight of his legend or the spark of something bigger. I was on edge, waiting to see how he'd respond.

After an ambitious but less-than-stellar attempt at professional baseball—because who doesn't wake up one day and decide to hit curveballs for a living?—Jordan returned to the Chicago Bulls. But instead of soaring triumphantly back to the top, he and his team were unceremoniously booted from the playoffs by the Orlando Magic. Some would say the biggest reason for the early exit was not because Michael Jordan was on the team, but rather because number 23 was not.

Critics sharpened their pens. Fans scratched their heads. Had the Jordan magic faded? Was Air Jordan now more of a Ground Jordan? I admit I read every headline, scanning for any hint of what Jordan would do next. My anticipation was fueled by a simple question: could even Michael Jordan come back from this?

For most people, this would be a sign to hang up the sneakers and maybe invest in a nice pair of golf clubs. But Michael wasn't most people. Instead of sulking or, heaven forbid, blaming his teammates (looking at you, every sore loser ever), Jordan took a hard look in the mirror.

He realized raw talent and a closet full of championship rings weren't enough. The game had evolved, and so must he. So instead of spending the off-season perfecting his blackjack strategy or filming yet another commercial, he dove back into training with a vengeance that would make Rocky Balboa look like a couch potato.

He didn't just practice; he redefined practice. Early mornings became his norm, sweat became his cologne, and the gym his second home. He studied the game, analyzed his opponents, and honed his skills to a razor's edge. He transformed his body, adapting to the new, more physical style of play that had emerged in his absence.

The result? The 1995–96 Bulls bulldozed their way into history with a 72–10 record—a feat so impressive that even the scoreboard needed a moment to catch its breath. Jordan reclaimed his throne, silenced the doubters, and added another championship to his collection. It wasn't magic; it was a method.

So what's the moral of this tale, besides confirming that Michael Jordan might actually be a basketball-playing cyborg? It's that excellence doesn't come from half measures or relying on past glories. It comes from a full-on, no-holds-barred commitment to being the best.

THE PIECEMEAL PITFALL

As financial advisors, we often find ourselves at similar crossroads. We want success, growth, and client satisfaction, but sometimes we're tempted to take shortcuts. We pick up the latest marketing gimmick here, a fancy software tool there, and sprinkle them into our existing routines like toppings on a mediocre pizza, hoping they'll somehow make the whole pie gourmet.

Spoiler alert: they won't.

I recall a time early in my career when I was guilty of this very approach. I'd latch on to the next shiny object—be it a trendy seminar, a flashy mailer, or a revolutionary cold-calling technique (yes, those were the days). I'd incorporate these tactics piecemeal into my practice, expecting them to magically elevate my business. But much like trying to fix a leaky boat with duct tape, the results were underwhelming at best.

It's like attempting to complete a jigsaw puzzle with pieces from different boxes. Sure, you might force a piece here or there, but the picture will be a distorted mess. To create a masterpiece, you need all the right pieces working together seamlessly.

THE ALL-IN MINDSET

What separates top performers from the rest isn't just talent. It's the commitment to go all in. Think about elite athletes across any sport—football, basketball, even those adrenaline-fueled F1 drivers who apparently have no concept of speed limits. They don't achieve greatness by dabbling. They dedicate themselves fully to their craft.

They practice relentlessly. Not just any practice, but deliberate, focused, and often grueling practice. They study the game, understand the rules inside and out, and constantly adapt to new challenges. They have a game plan for every scenario and execute it with precision.

I want to throw a bounce pass back to pro basketball here. I often think about Allen Iverson's infamous news conference rant, "We're talking about practice, man. Not a game. Practice."[4] While Iverson was

---

4   Allen Iverson, "Allen Iverson's Legendary Practice Rant [FULL] | ESPN Archives," May 7, 2002, posted May 7, 2019, by ESPN, YouTube, 30 min., 30 sec., https://www.youtube.com/watch?v=K9ZQhyOZCNE.

undoubtedly talented, his dismissal of practice highlighted a critical point: even the most gifted individuals can't rely on talent alone.

Financial advisors must adopt the same mentality. It's not enough to attend a workshop or purchase cutting-edge software like Simplicitree and expect miracles. You have to immerse yourself in it—understand it, practice it, live it. Half-hearted efforts yield half-baked results.

EXECUTING WITH EXCELLENCE

In our field, executing with excellence means committing to a comprehensive approach that integrates all aspects of your practice—client service, education, planning, and execution—into a cohesive whole.

Imagine you're preparing for a client meeting. You don't just glance at their plan five minutes before they walk in (or log on, in today's virtual world). You study their financial landscape, anticipate their questions, and prepare for anything to happen or come up. You practice using Simplicitree so it feels like the back of your hand, you refine your explanations and ensure you can educate by association in a way that's both engaging and understandable.

Look, it's easy to procrastinate, to tell ourselves we'll implement that new strategy "soon" or start practicing "when things slow down." But as the old saying goes, "The best time to plant a tree was twenty years ago. The second-best time is now."

Our work is about more than just being prepared; it's about striving for continuous improvement. Each client interaction is an opportunity to refine your skills. Pay attention to the questions they ask, the concerns they express, and use that feedback to enhance your approach.

Financial advisors must be willing to adapt, evolve, and put in the work that others would rather skip. The financial landscape is constantly changing—new regulations, market shifts, and technological advancements. To stay ahead, we need to be proactive, not reactive.

THE POWER OF COMMUNITY

Community matters. One of the most effective ways to foster excellence is by surrounding yourself with like-minded professionals. Engage with peers who are also committed to growth. Share insights, challenges, and successes. Not only does this create a support network, but it also pushes you to elevate your practice.

Think of it as a mastermind group for financial advisors—a place where iron sharpens iron and where the collective knowledge propels everyone forward. We do this in the form of a study group. We get our advisors together to study our business. Sometimes we even invite clients for a deeper understanding. More on this later.

PUTTING EVERYTHING TOGETHER

How do you avoid the piecemeal pitfall and execute with excellence? Here are some actionable steps:

1. **Commit Fully:** Decide to go all in. Embrace the tools, strategies, and practices that will enhance your business, and integrate them thoroughly.
2. **Practice Relentlessly:** Don't just familiarize yourself with new concepts—master them. Role-play client interactions, refine your presentations, and seek feedback. Ask a close friend or client to role-play with you. Ask them to point out holes in how you represent yourself. It will help you grow.
3. **Understand the Game:** Stay informed about industry changes, market trends, and regulatory updates. The more you know, the better you can serve your clients.
4. **Execute with Precision:** Develop a game plan for each client interaction and follow through. Consistency builds trust and credibility.
5. **Engage with Peers:** Join professional groups, attend conferences,

or create your network of advisors dedicated to excellence. Join one of our study groups. They are a blast and are designed to help you grow.

6. **Adapt and Evolve:** Be open to change. If something isn't working, don't be afraid to adjust your approach.

As financial advisors, we have the opportunity to make a profound impact on our clients' lives. But to do so effectively, we must be willing to invest in ourselves—our knowledge, our skills, and our practices.

So the question is, are you ready to lace up your sneakers, step onto the court, and go all in? Or will you settle for sitting on the bench, watching others play the game at a higher level?

The choice is yours. But remember, in the game of excellence, there are no shortcuts—only the rewards that come from dedication, practice, and a wholehearted commitment to being the best.

Now, if you'll excuse me, I have some practice to get to. After all, we're talking about practice, man. Practice.

Part 4

INVESTING IN MOTION

CHAPTER 13

NAVIGATING THE INVESTING ROLLER COASTER

Turn Stock Market Thrills into
Steady Dividend Rewards

It was the summer of 2000, and the air was thick with more than just humidity—it was buzzing with the kind of excitement that only a 310-foot steel monster can generate. My girlfriend and I, freshly off campus from our sophomore year, decided to celebrate our newfound freedom by tackling the Millennium Force at Cedar Point. This wasn't just any roller coaster; it was *the* roller coaster, the one that made other rides look like kiddie swings at a local fair.

The Millennium Force stood 310 feet tall, which was a record at the time, and boasted of speeds greater than ninety-three miles per hour. No other roller coaster had either of those stats, and we couldn't wait to get our turn to ride this thrilling roller coaster. We had learned shortly before getting in line that the Millennium Force wasn't going ninety-three miles an hour; it was being clocked at over one hundred miles per hour! Let's just say we couldn't wait for our turn to ride this rocket ship!

As we stood in line for over an hour, our anticipation grew with each step closer to the beast. We opted for the front seats because, of course, we wanted the full experience. Why settle for less when you're young and invincible? As the ride creaked upward, the world below shrank, and for a moment, I wondered if we could see our future from up here—a future full of possibilities, excitement, and maybe a few terrifying drops.

The clinking chain pulling us upward suddenly released, and we plummeted. Wind slapped my face like it had a vendetta.

"This is amazing!" I yelled, turning to share the moment, only to find that my girlfriend had passed out cold.

Not exactly the reaction I was hoping for. What started as the thrill of a lifetime quickly turned into a moment I would never forget, not because it was so amazing, but because it was so scary.

She came back to consciousness moments after passing out, but those moments seemed like years. After the coaster came to an end, we spent the rest of the day with our feet on the ground, firmly attached to the earth. It dawned on me that while I loved the adrenaline rush, she preferred her thrills a bit less…life-threatening. And that's okay.

Fast-forward to today. I find roller coasters make the perfect metaphor for investing and for how financial advisors guide our clients through the ups and downs of the market.

THE GREAT DEBATE: THRILL SEEKERS VERSUS STEADY CRUISERS

Just like amusement park enthusiasts, investors come in all shapes and sizes. Some are the Thrill Seekers, itching for the next big drop, the sharp turns, the zero-to-sixty-in-three-seconds kind of stocks. They're the ones who check their portfolios daily, maybe even hourly, reveling in the market's volatility like it's the latest action movie.

Then there are the Steady Cruisers, those who prefer the merry-go-round to the roller coaster. They're in it for the long haul, valuing stability over adrenaline. They want to enjoy the ride without the risk of losing their lunch—or their life savings.

Our job? To ensure each client gets on the ride that's right for them. And more often than not, especially with retirees or those nearing retirement, the Steady Cruisers approach is the way to go. That's where dividend investing comes into play.

DIVIDEND INVESTING: THE STEADY TREE THAT BEARS FRUIT

Dividend investing sounds about as exciting as watching paint dry, but hear me out. First, let's change the analogy. Instead of watching paint dry, think of dividend investing like planting a sturdy apple tree in your backyard.

Sure, it doesn't have the immediate thrill of buying a flashy new gadget or hopping on the latest investment craze. But season after season, that tree produces apples—tangible, reliable rewards you can count on.

While others chase fleeting trends that wither as quickly as they bloom, you're steadily filling your basket with fruit that keeps on giving. Let's break it down.

TEACHING CLIENTS IN REAL TIME

As I've mentioned a few times now, one of the most impactful things we can do as advisors is to educate our clients during the planning process, not after. Think about it. Would you trust a surgeon who didn't explain the procedure you needed to cure a disease until *after* you woke up from anesthesia? Probably not. You want to know what's wrong with your body, what they are going to do to fix it, what could go wrong, and what to expect after. Simply stated, you want to know everything.

Rather than crafting a masterpiece behind closed doors, involve your clients in building their investment strategy. Use tools like Simplicitree to show them in real time how their income shortfall can be addressed. When clients see that dreaded red number—the gap between their expected expenses and income—they feel that pit in their stomach. But when they participate in turning that red into green, filling the gap with reliable dividend income, they not only understand the plan—they own it.

DEMYSTIFYING DIVIDENDS WITH REAL-WORLD EXAMPLES

Nothing beats a good story, especially one that involves money. Let's take a utility company that's been paying dividends since 1942. That's through World War II, the moon landing, the invention of the internet, and every market hiccup in between. If a client had invested in this company twenty years ago, their dividend income would have increased every single year despite market volatility.

If you haven't noticed yet, I love to emphasize the importance of involving clients in the process. When I teach a client how dividends work, I use the following examples to demystify dividend investing. I don't just tell clients that dividends are reliable; I show them, using actual data from resources like Yahoo Finance, dividend websites, or similar tools that have information on dividend stocks.

This interactive approach turns a passive presentation into an engaging learning experience. Clients see dividends not as an abstract concept but as a tangible source of income that can weather market storms.

Black Hills Corporation (BKH)

- **Dividend History:** Paying dividends since 1942.
- **Dividend Growth:** In 2004, the dividend was $1.24 per share. By 2023, it increased to $2.60 per share.
- **Market Volatility:** Through the 2008 financial crisis, the 2020 pandemic, and other market downturns, Black Hills not only continued paying dividends but increased them.

For instance, I will pull up Black Hills Corporation, a company that's been paying dividends every year since 1942. I will point out the dividend rate—$2.60 per share—and then walk the client through this simple math:

Me: "Can you help me calculate how much dividend you would earn if you had 1,000 shares of Black Hills Corporation?

Client: "Yes, what do you need me to do?"

Me: "Take this calculator and multiply 1,000 shares by the dividend rate. How much was that again?"

Client: "The dividend rate on the screen says $2.60."

Me: "That's right, so take 1,000 shares and multiply that by 2.6 on the calculator."

Client: "That's $2,600."

Me: "That's right. You would get a check from Black Hills Corporation this year for $2,600 if you owned 1,000 shares of their stock."

Client: "What happens if the stock price drops?"

Me: "Great question. Even if the stock price fluctuates, as long as you hold those shares and the company maintains its dividend, you will get $2.60 for every share you own."

Or consider ExxonMobil, which has been paying dividends since 1882.

ExxonMobil (XOM)

- **Dividend History:** Paying dividends since 1882.
- **Dividend Rate:** Currently $3.80 per share.
- **Company Commitment:** Even during the 2020 pandemic, when oil prices plummeted, ExxonMobil maintained its dividend by cutting costs elsewhere.

Through pandemics, recessions, and whatever else history threw at us, their dividends kept coming.

When clients see these companies have been paying and increasing dividends for decades—even centuries—it builds confidence. They realize that dividend investing isn't some new, untested strategy. It's a tried-and-true method used by some of the wealthiest investors, like Warren Buffett and Bill Gates, who prioritize income-generating assets.

You can use all sorts of examples like these, as there are tons of them. I tend to change my examples from time to time, but one thing always remains the same—involving the client in the process of learning. I will always ask them to use a calculator and get involved.

ADDRESS COMMON CONCERNS WITH A SMILE

Clients often ask, "If this is so great, why isn't everyone doing it?" Well, not everyone likes roller coasters, remember? Many advisors focus on growth stocks and the thrill of the chase. Dividend investing might not be the flashiest game in town, but it's the one that lets clients sleep at night.

Another concern is market volatility. Clients worry if the stock price drops, their income will too. This is where you get to pull a rabbit out of your hat. Explain that dividends are paid per share, not based on the stock's current price. So unless the company cuts its dividend—a rarity for companies with a long history—their income remains steady.

Have you ever heard someone say, "I can't unsee that"? Or "I'll never forget that; it's burning into my memory"? Once you understand how dividend stocks work, you can't unlearn it. You will never see investing the same way again.

THE HUMOROUS SIDE OF SERIOUS INVESTING

Let's face it: finance can be drier than a saltine cracker in the Sahara. But who says it has to be? Adding a touch of humor can make even the most complex financial concepts easier to digest.

For example, when a client expresses concern about falling stock prices, you might respond, "Unless you're planning to sell all your shares and buy a private island, a temporary dip isn't the end of the world. And if you *are* buying an island, make sure there's space for a guest house!"

Or when explaining why some companies keep paying dividends, you could say, "Think of these companies like that friend who always insists on picking up the check. They just keep giving, and who are we to stop them?"

Humor can break the ice and make the conversation more engaging, but it's important to remember that these are real concerns deserving real answers. I may joke, but I'm committed to providing serious guidance and helping my clients understand their financial situation thoroughly. The key is to be genuine. What we do is serious and often challenging, so bringing some levity can help ease the tension. After all, people tend to learn more effectively when they're relaxed and comfortable.

THE POWER OF CONSISTENCY

Consistency is crucial—both in the dividends we seek and in the guidance we provide to our clients. By adhering to a strategy focused on reliable income, we help clients navigate market volatility without resorting to panic selling or hasty decisions.

It's like saying, "You don't jump off a roller coaster halfway through the ride just because it takes a sudden drop. You hold on, maybe scream a little, but you trust that it will smooth out again."

This is why I'm such a fan of dividends. It's not about convincing clients to stay invested during market downturns—many already understand that. But let's imagine they're tempted to sell everything. I'd ask, "If you needed your paycheck but hated your job, would you quit without another source of income lined up? How would you pay your bills?" When you retire, your money needs to work for you because something has to sustain your lifestyle. Consistency in income is what ensures that even when the ride gets bumpy, you can rely on a steady stream of support for your future.

PEACE OF MIND IN UNCERTAIN TIMES

Throughout my career, especially during periods of market volatility like the 2008 financial crisis or the 2020 pandemic, I've witnessed firsthand how dividend investing provides clients with peace of mind.

Instead of panicking over declining account values, clients focused on the steady income their investments continued to generate. I got a call from a client in May 2020, which was the bottom of the market for that year.

Here's what he asked me: "I have 100K in the bank right now… how fast can I get that to you to buy more dividends?" He understood that while the stock market was charging down the mountain, his dividend income remained on a smooth, predictable path. He just wanted to take advantage of the dip.

HELPING CLIENTS ENJOY THE RIDE

At the end of the day, our role is to match the ride to the rider. Not everyone wants the Millennium Force experience—in investing or life. And that's perfectly okay.

By educating our clients, involving them in the planning process, and injecting a bit of humor along the way, we empower them to make informed decisions. We transform the terrifying roller coaster of the market into a manageable, even enjoyable, journey.

So next time you're meeting with a client, remember: it's not just about the destination; it's about ensuring they enjoy the ride.

On that note, I have a lot to say about dividend investing…so much so that I'm going to stay on the topic in the next chapter. I'm going back to the beginning of my dividend journey to drive a few more points home.

Trust me on this: even if you're already familiar with dividend investing—plenty of advisors are—the next chapter offers new ways to help you tap into the mystique of dividend investing to get clients excited about it…even those thrill seekers.

CHAPTER 14

HOT TUB CONFESSIONS

*Dividend Epiphanies Can Surface
in Unexpected Places*

The sun was setting over the Pacific Ocean, casting a golden hue over the bustling streets of downtown San Diego. It was the perfect backdrop for the financial conference I was attending, but I had no idea that a casual conversation in a hot tub would forever change my approach to investing.

There we were, a group of financial advisors, all trying to unwind after a long day of sessions and networking. The steam rose around us as we swapped stories about markets and strategies, each of us convinced we had a good grasp of the investing world. That's when a close advisor friend, someone I respected for his depth of knowledge, casually mentioned something that made me sit up and listen.

"Dividends are the unsung heroes of investing," he said. "Most people don't understand their true power."

I nodded along, pretending to understand, but inside, I felt the embarrassment of how little I knew about dividend stocks at that moment. Here I was, well into my career as a financial advisor, and I realized I knew almost nothing about the nuances of dividend investing. I thought I knew about dividends—companies paid them out, investors got a little bonus, end of story. But as he peeled back the layers, explaining the intricacies of yield, payout ratios, and the dangers of chasing high yields without understanding the underlying fundamentals, it was as if a fog lifted.

He talked about the sustainability of dividends and how companies with a culture of consistent payouts would go to great lengths to maintain them, even in tough times. "Some companies," he said, "will cut thousands of jobs before they cut their dividends." His words painted a vivid picture of companies operating like families, fiercely protecting the source of their livelihood.

I sat there, the bubbles gurgling around me, as he described how dividends could act as an anchor in volatile markets, providing stability and peace of mind to investors. He spoke of the trap of high-yield stocks, which can be seductive but dangerous, much like fool's gold.

By the time I left that hot tub, I knew I had been missing something big. That night, I stayed up late, researching everything I could about dividends. It was the beginning of a new journey, one that would lead me to not just invest in dividend stocks, but to truly understand them. I learned to value not just the yield, but the company behind it—its history, its commitment, and its ability to weather storms.

It's funny how the simplest moments can become the most profound. For me, a casual conversation in a hot tub became the turning point in my career. It was a reminder that no matter how much we think we know, there is always more to learn. And sometimes the lessons come from the most unexpected places.

UNVEILING THE MYSTIQUE OF DIVIDEND INVESTING

Let's talk about the confusion behind dividend investing. I've mentioned dividend stocks and dividend portfolios throughout most of this book, so it's crucial to clear up some potential misunderstandings.

When I first began researching dividend stocks—well into my career, mind you—I was blown away by how little I knew.

I can still recall being in that hot tub in San Diego, feeling both relaxed and suddenly alarmed as I realized my knowledge gaps. I thought I knew what dividends were all about. Companies paid them, investors received a little extra cash—end of story, right? But as my fellow advisor friend unraveled the complexities, I thought, "Man, I don't know what those are about."

I don't want to assume you know everything about dividend stocks—after all, I certainly didn't. And I don't want to insult your intelligence. But let's be clear: when we're talking about dividend investing, we're not just chasing high-yield dividend stocks. There's a dangerous misconception that the higher the yield, the better the stock or opportunity. That couldn't be further from the truth.

THE FOOL'S GOLD OF HIGH YIELDS

High-yield dividend stocks can be seductive. Who wouldn't want a stock that pays out 10 percent, 15 percent, or even 20 percent? But much like fool's gold, these high yields can be deceptive and potentially disastrous if you don't understand what's behind them.

Imagine a stock priced at $100 per share, paying a 5 percent dividend—that's $5 per share. Now, suppose something goes wrong: the company makes bad decisions, and the stock price plummets to $50. The dividend is still $5 because it was declared before the drop, but now the yield appears to be 10 percent. To the untrained eye, this might seem like a fantastic opportunity. But is it?

If you didn't know the stock's history and saw a 10 percent yield, you might think, "This is a great deal!" But without understanding the company's fundamentals, you could be walking into a trap. High yields resulting from a falling stock price are often a red flag. That attractive yield can quickly become zero if the company cuts its dividend to survive.

To sum things up: high yields can be tempting, but they often come with higher risks. A company offering an unusually high dividend yield may be in financial trouble. It's essential to dig deeper and understand why the yield is high.

Remember, if it looks too good to be true, it probably is. High yields resulting from a declining stock price can quickly evaporate if the company cuts its dividend, a move that often leads to a further drop in stock price.

YIELD VERSUS DIVIDEND RATE: A CRUCIAL DISTINCTION

One of the first things to grasp is the difference between yield and dividend rate. Yield is volatile because it's a ratio of the stable dividend rate to the fluctuating stock price. When a stock price drops but the dividend remains the same, the yield increases. This can make a troubled stock look deceptively attractive if you're only looking at the yield percentage.

Understanding this distinction is vital. I didn't get it at first. I thought the dividend percentage would drop as the stock price dropped. But that's not how it works. The dividend is a fixed dollar amount declared by the company, and the yield fluctuates with the stock price.

THE INVESTMENT PHILOSOPHY: MORE THAN JUST HIGH YIELDS

When approaching a dividend portfolio, it's essential to focus on three key aspects:

1. **Stock Price Growth:** We want stocks with the potential to appreciate—a $100 stock that could become $200 or more.
2. **Dividend Income:** The stock should pay a consistent dividend, providing income regardless of market volatility.
3. **Growth of Dividend Income:** We aim for companies that not only pay dividends but also increase them over time, outpacing inflation.

We're not advocating for chasing after high-yield dividend stocks. Instead, we focus on the sustainability and growth potential of both the stock price and the dividends.

THE SHIFT BETWEEN TECH AND DIVIDENDS

Market dynamics often involve a "shift" between tech stocks and dividend-paying stocks. When the tech sector is booming, money flows out of stable, dividend-paying companies into high-growth tech stocks. Conversely, when tech falters, investors seek the safety of dividends.

Understanding this shift is crucial. Dividend portfolios tend to perform well when the broader market is doing poorly because investors flock to the stability and income that dividends provide. This dynamic highlights the anchoring effect of dividends in volatile markets. Understanding this relationship between tech stocks and value stocks has had a profound impact on how I manage client assets.

DIVIDENDS AS AN ANCHOR IN STORMY SEAS

A dividend is like an anchor in a turbulent market. Companies with a culture of paying dividends understand this and go to great lengths to maintain their payouts. They'll cut employee benefits, halt hiring, or even lay off staff before they reduce their dividends.

Why? Because they know that investors value the reliability of dividend income, especially during market downturns. This commitment to dividends provides peace of mind to investors and helps stabilize the stock price.

THE PSYCHOLOGICAL COMFORT OF DIVIDENDS

There's a psychological aspect to dividend investing that's often overlooked. When the market is volatile and stock prices are falling, investors in dividend-paying stocks still receive their dividend income. This consistent cash flow can alleviate the anxiety of market downturns.

Moreover, when stock prices are down, reinvested dividends buy more shares, setting the stage for greater gains when the market recovers. It's like getting your favorite pizza at half price—you get more slices for the same money.

THE ART OF MANAGING A DIVIDEND PORTFOLIO

Managing a dividend portfolio isn't about throwing darts at a board of high-yield stocks. It requires a deep understanding of each company's fundamentals. Here are some critical factors to consider:

1. UNDERSTAND WHAT THE COMPANY DOES

Before investing, make sure you understand the company's business model. What products or services do they offer? Are they in a sustainable and growing industry? Where is the company located, and who are their top competitors?

2. ASSESS THE DIVIDEND'S SUSTAINABILITY

Look at how long the company has been paying dividends. Has it increased its dividend over time without decreasing it over the same period of time? A history of consistent and growing dividends is a good indicator of financial health.

3. ANALYZE THE PAYOUT RATIO

The payout ratio is the percentage of earnings paid out as dividends. A lower payout ratio suggests the company has room to maintain or increase dividends. A payout ratio of over 100 percent or higher is a red flag—it means the company is paying out more in dividends than it's earning, which is unsustainable.

4. EXAMINE CASH FLOW

Cash flow is king. Review the company's cash flow statements to see how it manages its money. Is it generating enough cash to cover dividends? How much debt does it carry?

BUILDING A DIVIDEND PORTFOLIO THE RIGHT WAY

When constructing a dividend portfolio, focus on companies with:

- **Consistent Dividend Payments:** Companies that have a long history of paying and increasing dividends
- **Healthy Payout Ratios:** Generally between 40 percent and 60 percent, indicating that dividends are sustainable

- **Strong Cash Flow:** Companies that generate sufficient cash to cover dividends and invest in growth

Some investors might suggest buying into dividend aristocrats—companies that have increased dividends for twenty-five consecutive years or more. While these companies are stable, their dividend yields are often low, and their stock price growth may be limited due to their size.

Instead, look for companies that offer a balance between dividend yield and growth potential. This approach can provide both income and capital appreciation.

THE POWER OF REINVESTING DIVIDENDS

Reinvesting dividends can significantly enhance returns over time. It's the magic of compound interest at work—the "eighth wonder of the world," as Einstein reportedly said.

When you reinvest dividends, you're buying more shares. During market downturns, those dividends buy more shares at lower prices, positioning your portfolio for a stronger rebound when the market recovers.

DIRECT OWNERSHIP VERSUS FUNDS AND ETFS

Imagine you're at a buffet with all your favorite foods laid out: the perfectly cooked steak, creamy mashed potatoes, a vibrant salad bar, and, of course, a decadent dessert station. Now imagine you get to pick exactly what goes on your plate. You choose the best items, making sure each bite is exactly what you want and nothing that you don't. That's what direct ownership of dividend-paying stocks is like.

You get to hand-pick companies that align with your investment philosophy, creating a portfolio that's customized to your taste. If you value steady, predictable income, you might go for companies like Procter & Gamble or Johnson & Johnson, which have been paying and increasing dividends for decades. You're in control—no surprises, no hidden ingredients.

But now, let's consider a different scenario. You're still at the buffet, but this time, you have a chef making a plate for you. They pick a little bit of everything—some things you love, some things you're indifferent about, and maybe even a few things you'd rather not have at all. You don't get to choose what's on your plate; you're at the mercy of the chef's choices. That's what it can feel like investing in mutual funds or ETFs.

These funds bundle together a bunch of different stocks. It's like a mixed platter, and while it's diverse and generally well-balanced, it may not align with your taste or goals. Sure, you'll get some dividend-paying companies in the mix, but you're also likely to get some that don't align with your preference for steady income.

THE CASE OF THE DISAPPEARING DIVIDENDS

Take my friend, Dave, who loves his dividends. He's the guy who checks his mailbox every day, not because he's expecting a letter, but because he gets a kick out of receiving those dividend checks. He started investing in a dividend-focused ETF, thinking he'd get the same satisfaction he got from his individual stocks. But when the checks started coming in, something was off. They were smaller than he expected. What happened?

It turned out the fund wasn't passing all the dividends on to him. Some were kept back to cover management fees, and others were reinvested into companies that weren't paying dividends at all. Dave felt like he'd ordered a steak but was served a salad instead. He was getting some of what he wanted, but not the full experience.

THE HIDDEN COSTS OF A PREMADE PLATE

Speaking of that salad, let's talk about the dressing—or in this case, the management fees. When you invest in mutual funds or ETFs, you're paying someone to manage the portfolio for you. It's like paying a chef to prepare your meal. And while it might be convenient, it's not free. Even a small fee can take a big bite out of your returns over time.

I remember chatting with a client, Sarah, who had invested in a mutual fund for over twenty years. She thought she was doing great because the fund had grown steadily, and she'd reinvested all the dividends. But when we sat down to look at her statements, we realized the fees had eaten away at a significant portion of her returns—more than $50,000 over two decades! That's a lot of steak dinners.

THE CHEF'S PRIORITIES

Then there's the matter of the chef's—or, in this case, the fund manager's—priorities. When you own individual stocks, you can focus on long-term income, choosing companies that fit your strategy. But fund managers often have a different agenda. They're under pressure to show results every quarter, which can lead them to chase short-term gains rather than focusing on reliable dividend income.

It's like hiring a chef who's more interested in creating Instagram-worthy dishes than in making sure you leave the table satisfied. I had a client, Tom, who found this out the hard way. He invested in a fund that initially promised high dividend yields, but when the market took a downturn, the manager shifted investments to more growth-oriented stocks to protect the fund's performance metrics. Tom's dividends took a hit, and his carefully planned income stream was disrupted.

FLEXIBILITY: YOUR SECRET SAUCE

When you own your stocks directly, you can adapt as needed. You're like a home cook who can whip up a gourmet meal or keep it simple, depending on the ingredients on hand. Need to replace an underperforming stock? No problem. Want to take a little profit off the table and reinvest it in something with a higher yield? You got it.

I once helped a client, Nancy, who was widowed and relying on her dividend income. She had several solid stocks but felt she wasn't maximizing her income potential. Together, we reviewed her portfolio and swapped out a couple of lower-yielding companies for higher dividend payers. Her income increased by 15 percent that year, and she didn't have to worry about the fund manager's decisions disrupting her life.

THE LAST SCOOP

Direct ownership isn't for everyone. It requires time, knowledge, and a little bit of courage. But for those who want full control and the ability to savor every bit of their investments, it's a satisfying option. It's like cooking your favorite meal exactly how you like it, without relying on someone else's recipe.

Investing through funds or ETFs, on the other hand, is like eating out at a nice restaurant. It's convenient, and you get a wide variety of options, but you might not get the exact meal you had in mind. And that's okay too. For some, the convenience and diversification are worth it. But for those of us who want the full flavor of dividend investing, there's nothing like owning your slice of the pie.

Whether you're a chef in your kitchen or prefer to dine out, the important thing is knowing what's on your plate and how it got there. So next time you're deciding between direct ownership and a fund, think about what kind of meal you want to have. Because investing is a lot like eating well—it's all about enjoying the fruits of your labor.

EXECUTION IS EVERYTHING

Crafting a solid investment plan is vital, but execution is where the rubber meets the road. You can serve your clients well and plan meticulously, but if you manage portfolios poorly, the strategy falls apart.

As financial advisors, we must wear multiple hats—planner, educator, and portfolio manager. Each role is interconnected, and excelling in one area isn't enough. Our clients rely on us to guide them through market complexities, safeguard their assets, and help them achieve their financial goals.

EMBRACING CONTINUOUS LEARNING

Reflecting on my hot tub epiphany, I realize the journey of learning never ends. The financial world is ever evolving, and staying informed is crucial. Embrace curiosity. Ask questions. Dive deeper.

Whether you're a seasoned advisor or new to the field, there's always more to discover. And sometimes the most valuable insights come from unexpected places—even a casual conversation in a hot tub.

ADDING A DASH OF HUMOR

Before I wrap up, let's address the elephant in the room. Yes, I had a profound professional revelation in a hot tub. If that isn't the most California thing ever, I don't know what is. But hey, at least I didn't start wearing sandals to the office—or investing in avocado futures. Plot twist: I do wear sandals to the office. Remember, I love the beach, so palm tree polos, shorts, and sandals are pretty common in my office.

On a more serious note, remember that the path to expertise is paved with humility and a willingness to admit what we don't know. It's okay to feel out of your depth sometimes. After all, even the best swimmers can learn new strokes.

FINAL THOUGHTS ON DIVIDENDS

Dividend investing isn't just about collecting quarterly checks; it's about understanding the companies you're investing in and the role they play in your portfolio and your clients' lives. It's about balancing growth and income, risk and reward.

By focusing on the fundamentals, avoiding the allure of unsustainable high yields, and committing to continuous learning, we can build portfolios that weather storms and provide lasting value.

So let's roll up our sleeves, dive into the details, and maybe, just maybe, find our next big insight in the most unexpected place. Who knows? Perhaps the next epiphany awaits us—not in a hot tub this time—but in the ordinary moments when we choose to look a little closer.

CHAPTER 15

YOUR SECOND FIRST IMPRESSION

*Onboarding a Client Is Your
Second First Impression*

When my wife and I were approaching our tenth anniversary, I decided it was time to pull out all the stops. Usually, we plan our trips together, but this milestone deserved something extraordinary—something she'd never see coming. So, in a rare display of secrecy (and let's be honest, sheer bravery), I took the reins.

I tapped into my network of globe-trotting clients, seeking the perfect destination. That's when I first heard of a magical place called Little Palm Island, a secluded private island off the coast of the Florida Keys. According to his hush-hush tone and starry-eyed experiences, it was paradise personified: a luxurious spa, a world-class restaurant helmed by a chef with more awards than I have shorts, and an exclusivity level that made VIP sections look like public parks. It had only a handful of bungalows, ensuring privacy and an experience that couldn't be replicated.

I booked it immediately, patting myself on the back for what I was sure would be an unforgettable trip. But in the back of my mind, I couldn't shake the feeling: Had I oversold it to myself? Would the reality live up to the brochure-worthy mental images I'd constructed from my client's enthusiastic descriptions?

Fast-forward to the big reveal. We arrived at the mainland dock, and I was still keeping the destination under wraps. As we boarded the intimate boat that would ferry us to the island, I noticed my wife's eyes widening. Good start.

Upon arrival, we were greeted not just by the warm tropical breeze but by staff members who welcomed us by name. Now, I'm not talking about a casual glance at a clipboard followed by a forced smile. I mean genuine eye contact and a heartfelt "Welcome, Mr. and Mrs. Durso." It was as if we'd just come home from war overseas and our family was there to embrace us with signs, flowers, and so much excitement to see us.

Every time we strolled around the island, it was the same. Staff members we'd never met greeted us personally. I suspected they'd held secret meetings, passing around our photos like we were on a most-wanted list, albeit for hospitality rather than apprehension.

One afternoon, we decided to go to Key West for some shopping. The same boat that had brought us to the island was prepared exclusively for us—no crowds, no schedules, just us. When we reached the mainland, our car was not just waiting but staged. The doors were open, the engine was running, and two bottles of ice-cold water were placed in the cup holders as if they were Fabergé eggs. They'd even programmed the GPS to guide us to their sister hotel in Key West, where more surprises awaited.

Upon arrival at the sister hotel, we were again greeted by our names. They marked our car without us knowing, to allow the sister hotel to know who we were when we arrived. They offered us a room for the day, complete with a selection of swimsuits (in case we wanted to take a dip in the hotel pool), and informed us that they'd made reservations at several top-notch restaurants—our only dilemma was choosing which one. I half expected them to offer to chew my food for me; seriously, we were being treated like royalty, even though we are far from it.

By this point, I was convinced that if I casually mentioned a craving for some obscure tropical fruit, a staff member would shimmy up a tree and present it to me on a silver platter within minutes.

My initial expectations, inspired by my client's enthusiastic but perhaps insufficient description, were blown out of the water. What I experienced was not just a vacation but a masterclass in exceeding expectations. It was the personification of a second first impression, a concept that would soon redefine how I approached my business.

FROM SECOND FIRST IMPRESSION
TO LASTING RELATIONSHIPS

In the financial advisory world, securing a client often feels like the culmination of a long journey. You've had the meetings, crunched the numbers, addressed concerns, and finally they've decided to trust you with their financial future. But what if I told you this is just the beginning? Much like my experience at Little Palm Island, the real magic happens after a prospect signs the papers to become a client.

Most advisors are so excited to land a new client that they consider the job done. They move on to the next prospect, thinking the hard part is over. But this is where the typical advisor drops the ball. The biggest opportunity we have to make a lasting impression isn't during the initial courtship; it's during that crucial first meeting after they've become a client. This is our chance to deliver a second first impression—one that solidifies the relationship and sets the tone for years to come.

THE LULL BETWEEN DECISION AND ACTION

Think about the period right after a client signs on. There's often a lull—a quiet stretch where assets are being transferred, paperwork is processed, and not much seems to be happening from the client's perspective. This can take anywhere from three to six weeks. During this time, the initial excitement can wane, and doubts may creep in. The client might wonder, "Did I make the right choice? Why haven't I heard from my advisor?"

This period is similar to the anticipation I felt before arriving at Little Palm Island. My initial impression was based solely on someone else's description. It wasn't until I experienced the exceptional service firsthand that my expectations were not just met but greatly exceeded.

As advisors, we have a golden opportunity during this waiting period to reinforce the client's decision. Instead of letting the relationship cool off, we can use this time to deepen the connection, educate them further, and make them feel valued.

ELEVATING THE ONBOARDING EXPERIENCE

How do we turn this potential lull into a moment of magic? By transforming the onboarding process from a mundane administrative step into an engaging, educational, and empowering experience.

Most advisors treat onboarding as a mere formality—a quick handoff to an assistant or an email with paperwork to fill out. But imagine if, instead, we made this first postsigning meeting all about the client, ensuring they understand every facet of their investment and feel genuinely excited about the journey ahead.

WALKING THROUGH THE STATEMENT JUNGLE

I recall a conversation with an advisor who attended a study group years ago. He boasted about having twelve meetings to onboard a client. Twelve! I thought he might have been counting coffee breaks and restroom visits in that number. But he was onto something—clients crave understanding.

So I decided to make the first postsigning meeting all about demystifying the client's statement. Yes, the dreaded, convoluted, jargon-filled statement that usually ends up in a drawer—or the fireplace.

I sit down with clients, statement in hand, and we walk through it together, line by line. I hand them a calculator—not because I can't do the math, but because I want them to feel the numbers. We start with the basics: the number of shares they own, the market price, and the value of their investment. Then we delve into the exciting world of dividends.

If you remember back a few chapters, I used this same technique when I introduced them to dividends. This time, I am doing it for real with their stock dividend shares, and it's much more personal.

"See this dividend rate?" I ask, pointing to a figure often overlooked. "That's how much you get paid per share. Let's do some quick math."

I let them punch in the numbers: number of shares multiplied by the dividend rate. Eyes widen as they see their estimated annual income materialize on the calculator screen.

"Wait, I get this much just for holding the stock?" they ask.

"Exactly," I reply. "And here's the best part—this company has been paying its dividends since 1882. Through wars, recessions, and market crashes, they've consistently paid—and often increased—their dividends."

I flip back to historical data, showing them how dividends have grown over time, even when stock prices fluctuated. We discuss market downturns not as doom-and-gloom scenarios, but as opportunities.

Similarly, clients often fear they've bought in at the top of the market. "What if I invest now and the market tanks tomorrow?" they ask.

"Great question," you respond. "Let's assume you bought at the very top, and the market drops the next day. While the value of your shares may decrease in the short term, your dividend income remains the same—as long as you hold on to your shares."

You might even illustrate this with historical examples. "In 2008, during the financial crisis, many stock prices plummeted. But companies like this one not only continued to pay dividends but increased them the following year."

ACTIVE PARTICIPATION: THE KEY TO UNDERSTANDING

I've covered this topic at different times throughout the book, but this is a good time to bring it back into the mix. Throughout this process, I make sure my client is the one doing the calculations. There's something powerful about physically entering numbers and seeing results firsthand. It's like teaching someone to fish rather than handing them a meal.

I recall one client fumbling with the calculator, laughing nervously. "I'm not great with numbers," they admitted.

"Perfect," I said. "That means you won't have any bad habits to unlearn."

By the third example, they were confidently crunching numbers, asking insightful questions, and—most importantly—understanding their investment on a deeper level.

THE SECOND FIRST IMPRESSION IN ACTION

This onboarding meeting transforms the client's experience. Right in front of them, we are using their statement, running some calculations, and connecting back to their Simplicitree plan. Like magic, it all comes into focus, and they can see how everything is connecting together. They've gone from passively nodding along in meetings to actively engaging with their financial future. They're not just clients anymore; they're partners.

And much like the staff at Little Palm Island knew my name and anticipated my needs, we're showing our clients we know them, we value them, and we're committed to exceeding their expectations.

The results have been astounding. Clients leave the onboarding meeting excited, empowered, and eager to share their experience. They tell their friends and family, "You have to meet my advisor. He makes sense of all this financial stuff and makes it fun!" For the first time, it's an experience clients won't forget.

I've had new clients walk in saying, "I hear you're going to make me use a calculator," with a grin on their face. The second first impression not only solidifies our relationship with existing clients, but it also opens the door to new ones.

BEYOND THE STATEMENT: EMBRACING TECHNOLOGY

In today's digital age, clients receive electronic statements, often buried behind login screens and passwords they can't remember. Part of our onboarding process involves walking them through their online account. We help them log in, navigate the interface, and find the information that matters most to them.

It's not uncommon for clients to marvel at features they've never seen before. "I had no idea I could see my projected income for the year laid out like this!" they exclaim.

By empowering clients to use these tools, we're giving them control and confidence. They no longer feel like passive observers but active participants in their financial journey.

CREATING A LASTING IMPACT

The second first impression is about more than just a meeting. It's about redefining the client-advisor relationship. We're not just managing their money; we're educating and empowering them. We're turning confusion into clarity, fear into confidence.

Much like my experience on Little Palm Island, where every detail was meticulously crafted to exceed expectations, our onboarding process is designed to surprise and delight our clients. We're showing them that their decision to work with us wasn't just good—it was the best decision they could have made.

COMMITMENT, COURAGE, AND GROWTH

Implementing this process requires commitment and courage. It's not the industry norm, and it takes time and effort. But the growth—both for our clients and our practice—is worth it.

We've moved away from chasing the next big marketing gimmick or marketing program. Instead, we're focused on serving with excellence and creating unforgettable experiences for our clients.

Onboarding isn't just a procedural step; it's an opportunity to make a profound impact. By taking the time to educate and engage our clients, we're not only enhancing their experience but also enriching our practice.

Remember, the first impression may get them in the door, but it's the second first impression that turns them into lifelong advocates.

So hand them the calculator, walk them through their statement, and watch as they transform from uncertain newcomers to confident partners in their financial future.

After all, anyone can make a first impression, but making a memorable second first impression—that's where the real magic happens.

CHAPTER 16

CONSISTENCY IS KING

*Revisit Fundamentals to Reinforce
Trust and Drive Lasting Success*

Are you ready for more sports? Great—because I can't help myself here. Let me start with a quiz question: What do Michael Jordan, Tom Brady, and Kurt Warner have in common? Sure, you might say they're all champions, MVPs, and household names in their respective sports. But dig a little deeper, and you'll find a more compelling thread weaving their stories together.

I still remember the first time I heard how Michael Jordan was cut from his high school basketball team in tenth grade. I thought, "You've got to be kidding. MJ got cut?" It was a gut punch that could have ended his hoop dreams right then and there. The Tom Brady story similarly caught my attention. Picked at 199th overall, he might as well have been a no-name—sitting on the bench, just waiting for a chance. And then there's Kurt Warner, who wasn't even drafted; I can still picture reading about how he was bagging groceries before he made it big. Talk about stories that make you do a double take.

Each of these legendary athletes wasn't always great. They struggled mightily at the start of their careers. And every time I revisit their backstories, I catch myself shaking my head in awe of how easily their trajectories could have been entirely different. But how did they transform from underdogs to icons? It wasn't just raw talent or a lucky break. It was their relentless commitment to practicing the fundamentals. They didn't rest on their athletic abilities; they honed them. They watched game film until their eyes blurred, studied their opponents' tendencies, and never stopped refining their craft—even after tasting success.

These athletes adapted to changes in the game, just as financial advisors and clients must adapt to shifting economic landscapes. Yet, amid all the adaptations, they never abandoned the basics. They understood that fundamentals aren't just for beginners; they're the bedrock of sustained excellence. I think about that every time a new hotshot prospect enters the league. Talent is one thing, but the grind of perfecting the basics is what separates the one-hit wonders from the all-time greats.

As financial advisors, we can learn a lot from their journeys. The annual review process isn't just a routine check-in or a progress report. It's an opportunity to revisit and reinforce the core principles that got your clients to where they are today. It's about starting over, diving back into the basics, and ensuring that both you and your clients are aligned and prepared to adapt to whatever comes next.

Just like the practice space of those legendary athletes had, the client review is our practice field—a place where we revisit the fundamentals, adapt to new challenges, and reinforce the strategies that drive success. I try to remind myself of that every time I crack open a client file for review. It might seem routine, but it's the same mindset that turned a grocery clerk into a Hall of Fame quarterback. And if that doesn't inspire you to go the extra mile, nothing will.

THE IMPORTANCE OF THE CLIENT REVIEW

I've written about the importance of the client review throughout this book. Now it's time to dig into what happens when we sit down with a client.

Think about all the first impressions you might have made after a year of working with a client: when they first visited your website, when they sat down with you for the initial consultation, when they navigated your financial planning software (I'll refer to Simplicitree again for the sake of discussion).

By the time we reach the first full-year review, we've probably met with them four, five, maybe even six times. In the first year alone, we're sitting down with them quite often, establishing a cadence that builds trust and familiarity.

Here's the kicker: after that initial flurry of meetings, there's usually a lull of six months, maybe more. When they come back in, a lot has happened, both in their lives and in the market. Our job is to catch up, recalibrate, and reengage.

REPETITION IS ESSENTIAL

Before we delve deeper into the client review process, let's pause to consider a fundamental psychological concept that profoundly impacts our work—and one I've mentioned before: the forgetting curve. If you've already forgotten about the forgetting curve, you can either go back to Chapter 5 for a refresher or keep reading. (Seriously, though, if you've forgotten about it, you're helping to validate my point.)

Here's the refresher course:

- The forgetting curve illustrates how we lose information over time when we don't attempt to retain it.
- In simple terms, we forget things rapidly.

- Within an hour, people forget an average of 50 percent of new information they've encountered.
- After twenty-four hours, they forget about 70 percent.
- After a week, it's up to 90 percent.

In our profession, we live and breathe what we do daily…and we're not immune to forgetting. How many times have you had to look up something you thought you knew by heart? Or revisit a financial strategy because the details got a bit fuzzy?

We attend conferences, webinars, and training sessions, absorbing a wealth of information. Yet without regular reinforcement, much of that knowledge slips away like sand through our fingers. If we—who engage with financial concepts every day can forget, imagine how our clients feel.

CLIENTS FACE AN UPHILL BATTLE

Our clients sit down with us a few times a year, maybe even less. They're exposed to complex financial concepts that are often entirely new to them. They might grasp the ideas during the meeting, nodding along and asking insightful questions. But once they walk out the door, the forgetting curve starts its silent work.

By the time they get home, they've forgotten half of what we discussed. A week later, only fragments remain. When the market takes a turn or their neighbor boasts about a hot stock tip, confusion sets in. They can't recall the fundamentals we painstakingly explained, leaving them vulnerable to doubt and fear.

BRIDGING THE GAP WITH REPETITION

Repetition is the antidote to the forgetting curve. Each time we revisit the core elements of their financial plan, we reinforce their understanding and help transfer information from short-term to long-term memory. This is the reason for the annual review—or more accurately, the regular review. It isn't just a procedural formality. It's a necessity.

It's like building muscle. You don't go to the gym once and expect to be fit for life. It takes consistent effort over time. Similarly, by regularly reviewing their financial plan, we help clients strengthen their financial literacy muscles.

ENHANCE RETENTION THROUGH ENGAGEMENT

Engaging clients actively in the review process boosts retention. When clients participate—taking control of the keyboard, updating their data, asking questions—they're more likely to remember the information. Active involvement transforms them from passive recipients to active learners.

Repetition doesn't just benefit clients; it helps us as advisors too. Each review reinforces our understanding of the client's unique situation. It reminds us of their goals and concerns and the strategies we've put in place. This continuous reinforcement ensures we're providing the most relevant and effective advice.

Instead of viewing the forgetting curve as a hurdle, see it as an opportunity. Each meeting is a chance to reconnect, reeducate, and reinforce. By acknowledging that forgetting is a natural human tendency, we can tailor our approach to mitigate its effects.

GETTING DOWN TO BUSINESS

Here are some questions we all should ask our clients:

- What's changed in your life?
- Have you lost a job?
- Are you still planning to retire at sixty-five?

- Have you decided sixty is the new sixty-five?
- Did you decide to sell everything and move to Bali to start an alpaca farm?

Okay, maybe the last one is a bit of a stretch, but you get the point: life changes can significantly adjust their financial plan. We need to know about them, preferably before clients invest their retirement savings in exotic livestock.

Some clients leave stuff out. They'll casually mention, "Oh, we replaced the roof, so we took out $50,000 from our account." Wait, what? When did this happen? Or they'll say, "We inherited some money, but we didn't want to bother you with it." Folks, this is what we're here for! We're part of this journey, not just the pit stops.

UPDATING FINANCIAL ACCOUNTS

After discussing life changes, we need to update financial accounts. Have they opened new credit lines, acquired new assets, or taken on new liabilities? Remember, clients might not think to inform us about every financial move they make—sometimes because they don't want to bother us and sometimes because they don't realize its impact.

One of my colleagues mentioned a client who casually said they took out a significant sum for home renovations without informing us. This isn't just about courtesy; such actions can affect their financial plan significantly. Our role is to help them understand the implications of these decisions and adjust their plan accordingly.

IT'S ALL ABOUT THE SHORTFALL

Remember all that business about the shortfall from Chapter 7? In celebration of repetition, let's have another run at it.

One of the most important things we can do right out of the gate is go over their shortfall again. It's easy to assume that once we've explained something—even if we've involved them in the process—they've got it locked down. But let's face it: we're the ones doing this every day, all day. They're in our office for a couple of hours a year. Expecting them to remember every detail is like expecting me to remember where I left my car keys after a long day—optimistic at best.

We have to bring them back to the core of their financial plan, the basics that define their path to success. This isn't just about reviewing numbers; it's about reinforcing understanding.

ADDRESSING ANY ELEPHANTS IN THE ROOM

Sometimes clients come in with preconceived notions, emotions, or expectations. They might have been chatting with friends who boast about their portfolios "crushing it" (usually based on that one hot stock pick they won't stop talking about). They're bombarded with media messages about the market soaring or plummeting, and they start to wonder, "Why am I not seeing those kinds of returns?"

This is where we need to ground them back in reality—their reality. We pull up their financial plan in Simplicitree and revisit their specific benchmark. Not the S&P 500, not the Nasdaq—their benchmark, based on their goals, needs, and risk tolerance.

THE BENCHMARK THAT MATTERS

Let's be clear. The S&P doesn't know who you are. The Nasdaq isn't aware of their retirement dreams or the fact that they want to buy a beach house in five years. Their benchmark is the one we created together, tailored to their unique situation.

By bringing them back to this personalized benchmark, we help them avoid the pitfalls of comparison. As Theodore Roosevelt is commonly credited with saying, "Comparison is the thief of joy." Or, in the financial world, "Comparison is the thief of rational investment decisions."

DEALING WITH FOMO (FEAR OF MISSING OUT)

Ah, FOMO—the bane of every investor's existence. When the market's taken off and growth stocks are skyrocketing, clients might feel like they're missing out. They see headlines about companies like NVIDIA (no, not the latest energy drink), and they wonder why their portfolio isn't doubling overnight.

We have to remind them that chasing the hottest stocks is a bit like trying to catch a greased pig at a county fair—not advisable and likely to end poorly.

MORE ON THE REALITY OF DIVIDENDS

Have I bored you enough about dividends yet? I hope not. Here's more.

Dividend stocks might not always be the life of the party, but over time, they've shown remarkable resilience and performance. There are periods when they underperform compared to flashy growth stocks, but history shows that dividends have outperformed growth stocks by an average of 4.1 percent per year over the long haul. That's not just winning the race; that's lapping the competition while sipping a cup of coffee.

I once had clients who were secretly comparing our dividend portfolio to the best dividend mutual fund Vanguard had to offer. For over a year, they measured our performance, dividends, and fees against Vanguard's best. When they finally revealed this covert operation, I braced myself for bad news. Instead, they told me we'd beaten Vanguard across the board—even after accounting for our "higher" fees.

I felt like I'd just won an Oscar, minus the awkward acceptance speech and the risk of being played off the stage by music.

THE POWER OF CONSISTENCY

Jordan…Brady…Warner…they each stuck to the fundamentals. What about you? What game are you playing? Does it emphasize the importance of a consistent investment strategy?

There are times when dividend stocks, those lovely "boring" investments, may underperform compared to flashy growth stocks. But over time, dividends have shown remarkable resilience and performance.

We need to bring clients back to the basics every time we meet. This isn't about being redundant; it's about reinforcing the core principles that will lead them to their financial goals.

GROUNDING OURSELVES AND OUR CLIENTS

Let's not forget that we can get caught up in the emotional whirlwind of the markets too. There are days when I walk into an advisor's office, exasperated, wondering why our portfolios aren't performing as well as the high-flying tech stocks everyone's raving about.

But then I remind myself—and my clients—our strategy isn't about chasing the next big thing. It's about building sustainable wealth over time, focusing on reliable income through dividends, and aligning with each client's specific goals.

MEETING CADENCE AND CLIENT ENGAGEMENT

Another crucial aspect is meeting cadence. In the early years, clients often want to meet frequently—every three months or so. And while the introvert in me might cringe at the thought of so many meetings, this is where we build trust and reinforce our value.

Over time, the frequency naturally decreases as clients become more comfortable and confident in the plan. But we should never assume that less frequent meetings mean less engagement.

Always schedule the next meeting before they leave your office, even if it's eighteen months out. It's like making a dentist appointment—you might not look forward to it, but it's important for long-term health (and you get a free toothbrush).

Allowing clients to decide the frequency of meetings gives them ownership of the process. It enhances their comfort level and ensures they're getting the support they need. Some may want to meet more frequently; others may feel an annual review suffices. The key is to be flexible and responsive to their needs.

THE ORGANIC UNFOLDING OF NEW NEEDS

During these reviews, new needs often surface organically. Maybe they want to discuss estate planning or long-term care, or that alpaca farm idea is gaining traction. By being patient and letting the conversation unfold naturally, we can address these needs without pushing our agenda.

It's not about chasing revenue; it's about providing value. And when clients feel valued and heard, the revenue follows.

AVOIDING THE HARD SELL

In the past, I used to be very methodical about introducing topics like Roth conversions, life insurance, and estate planning. While these are important, I've learned that forcing these discussions can make clients feel like they're being sold to rather than advised.

Now I let these topics emerge organically. If a client brings up concerns about long-term care, we dive into it. If they mention wanting to leave a legacy for their grandchildren, we discuss estate planning options. This approach builds trust and demonstrates we're attentive to their priorities, not just our own.

CLIENT REVIEWS EQUALS CUSTOMER EXPERIENCE

The way you handle reviews shouldn't be about just ticking a box off or a mundane obligation. Reviews are opportunities to revisit the fundamentals, reinforce the strategies that work, and adapt to any changes in the client's life or the market.

Just like the greatest athletes who continually practiced the basics, we must return to the core principles that drive success in our clients' financial lives. By doing so, we not only empower them but also reaffirm our role as trusted advisors.

Here are some final tips to lead us out:

- Throughout the process, maintaining a consistent message is crucial. From the first meeting to the tenth annual review, the core principles remain the same. This consistency reinforces trust and helps clients internalize the strategies we've set in place.
- Tools like Simplicitree enhance this process by providing visual representations of their financial plans, shortfalls, and benchmarks. By involving clients in updating their data—letting them take control of the keyboard or mouse—we engage them in a co-planning environment. This hands-on approach deepens their understanding and commitment to the plan.
- Finally, remember the client review is more than just a meeting. It's a pivotal part of the customer experience. It's where clients take ownership of their plan and don't forget why they chose to work with us in the first place. By consistently revisiting the fundamentals and engaging clients in the process, we're not only solidifying our relationship but also setting the stage for organic growth and referrals.

The next time you sit down for a client review, remember: this isn't just about numbers on a page. It's about reigniting the passion for the fundamentals, embracing the power of repetition, and maybe, just maybe, helping your client avoid investing in that alpaca farm.

Part 5

PAIRING PROFESSIONAL COMPETENCE WITH CLIENT COMPASSION

CHAPTER 17

EXPERTISE + EMPATHY = SUCCESS

Let Your Client See Their Entire Financial Story

I never imagined a simple cough could flip my world upside down. It all started innocently enough—I developed a persistent cough just before a mission trip to Kenya. Knowing that healthcare options might be limited there, I visited my doctor beforehand. He chalked it up to allergies or postnasal drip, handed me some meds, and sent me on my way.

Off I went to Kenya, meds in tow, but my cough only worsened. The pills provided temporary relief, but nothing substantial. Upon returning home, I had less than twenty-four hours before jetting off to Hawaii for a two-week family vacation. Paradise awaited, but so did a worsening cough that had me hacking up blood.

A trip to urgent care led to a whirlwind of events. One moment, we were joking about getting back to the beach; the next, a doctor was pointing at a spot on my lung X-ray and saying words no one wants to hear: "That's not good. It could be a tumor, cancer, or tuberculosis. You need to go to the ER right now."

Suddenly, my life was a medical drama. Admitted to the hospital and isolated due to the potential of tuberculosis, I was poked, prodded, and subjected to a battery of tests. Specialists paraded in and out, each more concerned about containing a disease than addressing my mounting fears. They were focused on their protocols, not on me.

After three and a half days—and an astronomical medical bill—the verdict was in: an atypical bacterial infection that required just fifty-two dollars' worth of antibiotics. All that chaos for something so potentially easy to heal. I am not trying to lessen the seriousness of my health issue, but rather highlight the reality I faced.

The experience left a sour taste, to say the least. The doctors were so intent on ruling out their worst-case scenarios that they forgot about the person behind the symptoms. They controlled the narrative, leaving me in the dark, anxious, and unheard.

This ordeal taught me a valuable lesson: the importance of controlling the narrative and staying attuned to the needs of those we serve. The doctors had their agenda, their checklist of things to rule out, but they failed to communicate with me effectively. They didn't consider my perspective, my fears, or my need for information.

As financial advisors, we must avoid this pitfall. Our clients come to us with fears, hopes, and uncertainties. If we impose our agenda without truly listening, we risk alienating them. Just like those doctors, we might be experts in our field, but expertise without empathy is a prescription for failure.

THE ADVISOR'S IMPERATIVE

One of the biggest challenges advisors face is maintaining a consistent message with clients. We're adept at crafting financial plans and investment strategies, but when it comes to implementation and execution, the narrative can get muddled.

Why? Because once clients leave our office or close their laptops, we lose control over the information they consume. They receive statements from the custodians that hold their money—statements designed to satisfy IRS requirements and make CPAs happy, but not necessarily to reflect the value we bring to the table.

THE CUSTODIAL CONUNDRUM

Custodial statements focus heavily on cost basis and account value, but they often overlook crucial elements like historical deposits, historical withdrawals, and the income generated from dividends and interest year over year. This creates a disconnect between what the client sees and what we've done for them.

Imagine a client who regularly contributes to their 401(k) noticing their retirement account seems to be growing faster than the portfolio you manage. They might think, "Why isn't my account performing as well?" They forget they're pumping thousands of dollars annually into their 401(k), skewing the apparent growth. It's like comparing apples to oranges—or perhaps apples to Apple stock.

THE COST BASIS CONUNDRUM

Cost basis can be a tricky beast. In dividend-focused strategies, reinvested dividends increase the cost basis over time. So a client who initially invested $1 million might see a cost basis of $1.25 million after several years of reinvestments. They might scratch their heads and wonder why their account hasn't grown as much as expected, not realizing the increased cost basis reflects reinvested earnings, not additional out-of-pocket investments. The client only added $1 million, not $1.25 million, but the statement doesn't reflect that.

I had a young client roll over a $19,000 IRA. A few years later, their statement showed a cost basis of $30,000 with a market value of $34,000. They were puzzled. "Did I somehow invest more money without knowing it?" they asked. It took a detailed explanation to clarify how reinvested dividends had increased their cost basis.

THE INCOME INVISIBLE MAN

Another issue is how statements handle income tracking—or rather, how they don't. Clients are often keenly interested in the income their portfolios generate, especially when we're solving for their retirement shortfall. Yet custodial statements rarely provide a clear history of dividends and interest earned. It's like trying to watch a movie with half the scenes missing.

Statements are excellent at showing the account value, sometimes six to nine times on the overview page. They want clients to focus on that one figure. But from an income planner's standpoint, the focus should be on income because we're solving for their shortfall. The lack of income history is a significant gap in the narrative.

THE TALE OF THE MISSING MILLIONS

Let me share a story that drove this point home for me. A client called me in a panic, upset about significant losses in their account. According to their online statement, their account value had dropped dramatically. I was baffled. Our portfolios over that period hadn't taken a nosedive.

After some digging, I realized the custodian's website showed the highest daily account value without accounting for substantial withdrawals the client had made. They had deposited large sums and then withdrawn hundreds of thousands of dollars within the same year. The statement didn't reflect these withdrawals, making it seem like the account had lost money when, in fact, the client had simply spent it.

Same situation, different client. A new client opened a non-IRA account and deposited $1.4 million into it. A month later, the client added $500,000 to that account from the sale of a home. A month after that deposit, she took $500,000 out of her account and bought another home. Fast-forward to eight months later during a review. The client asked me why she had lost money when it looked like all of her stocks were up. A bit baffled, I looked into it. The custodian didn't account for the $500,000 withdrawal. We had made her $250,000 in gains, but her account was showing a $250,000 loss because of her $500,000 deposit that she took back out.

This misunderstanding could have been avoided if the statements provided a clearer narrative. But since they didn't, I had to step in and reconstruct the story. Super frustrating.

INTRODUCING THE SNAPSHOT: REWRITING THE NARRATIVE

Frustrated by these recurring issues, we decided to take matters into our own hands. We developed a tool we call the "Snapshot." Admittedly, it's not the most creative name, but it serves its purpose. It captures the essential elements that clients care about in one concise document.

The Snapshot focuses on four key metrics:

1. **Deposits:** How much money has the client deposited over time?
2. **Withdrawals:** How much have they taken out?
3. **Dividend and Interest Income:** How much income has the portfolio generated?
4. **Account Value:** What's the current value of the account?

By presenting this information year by year, we create a narrative that aligns with the client's experience and our strategic objectives. This system allows a client to view their entire history on a single page. It's a great picture to show an advisor's real value; after all, we are more than a great smile.

BREAKING DOWN THE FOUR METRICS

Let's dive deeper into these four critical components and understand why they matter so much to both us and our clients.

1. Deposits: The Forgotten Contributions

Clients often forget how much they've invested over the years. They might remember the initial deposit but lose track of subsequent contributions. This can lead to misunderstandings when they compare their cost basis to their account value.

For example, a client might say, "I invested $500,000 with you, but my account is only worth $600,000. That's just a 20 percent gain over several years." But they might be forgetting the additional $100,000 they've contributed over time. The Snapshot helps them see the total deposits, providing a clearer picture of their investment journey. This is a horrible example, I know, but it might be the truth.

2. Withdrawals: The Invisible Spending

Withdrawals are another area where memory can be selective, or the most selective. Clients often forget how much they've taken out, especially if withdrawals were spread out over several years or used for various purposes like vacations, home renovations, or helping family members.

I had a client who had withdrawn over $700,000 in three years but was concerned that their account hadn't grown much. Without accounting for these withdrawals, it would seem like poor performance. The Snapshot brings these figures to light, reminding clients of their spending and its impact on their portfolio.

3. Dividend and Interest Income: Unsung Heroes

Dividends and interest are the engine that powers many of our clients' portfolios, especially those focused on income generation. Yet standard statements rarely highlight this critical component.

Consider a client who invested $433,000 with us. In the first year, their portfolio generated $10,000 in dividends. Fast-forward several years, and it's now generating $44,000 annually. That's a 440 percent increase in income without additional deposits. The Snapshot showcases this growth, reinforcing the value of our dividend-focused strategy. Yet most, if not all, custodial statements don't highlight this at all, and even worse, it would take a true mathematician to figure it out on the custodian's website.

4. Account Value: More than Just a Number

While account value is important, it doesn't tell the whole story. Market fluctuations, deposits, withdrawals, and reinvested dividends all affect this number. By presenting account value alongside the other three metrics, we provide context that helps clients understand their true financial position.

THE POWER OF REBALANCING

An interesting insight we've gained from using the Snapshot is the positive impact of rebalancing, especially when clients make significant withdrawals.

Clients who frequently withdraw funds force us to rebalance their portfolios more often. This regular rebalancing can lead to better performance because it involves selling overvalued assets and buying undervalued ones—a classic "buy low, sell high" strategy.

For example, a client who withdrew $1.3 million over several years still saw their account value grow from $4 million to $5.3 million.

The act of rebalancing during these withdrawals contributed to this growth.

ALIGNING THE SNAPSHOT WITH THE CLIENT'S JOURNEY

The Snapshot isn't just a tool for us; it's a mirror reflecting the client's financial journey. It ties together their deposits, withdrawals, income generation, and account value in a way that's easy to understand.

When clients see their financial history laid out like this, it often leads to moments of realization. They appreciate the growth in their dividend income, understand the impact of their spending, and see how their portfolio has performed over time.

THE IMPORTANCE OF MEMORY AND PERCEPTION

Memory is a funny thing. Clients might not remember withdrawing significant amounts, especially if those withdrawals were used for nonrecurring expenses. They might also forget about additional deposits or how their dividend income has grown.

By controlling the narrative with the Snapshot, we help bridge the gap between perception and reality. We provide a factual account that can alleviate concerns and reinforce trust.

DEALING WITH CLIENT CONCERNS

Let's revisit the story of the client who thought they had lost money due to the custodian's misleading account value display. Without the Snapshot, addressing their concerns would have been challenging.

With the Snapshot in hand, I could show them:

- **Deposits:** The total amount they had invested over the years
- **Withdrawals:** The significant amounts they had taken out
- **Dividend Income:** The income their portfolio had generated
- **Account Value:** How their account value had grown despite withdrawals

This comprehensive view helped them understand they hadn't lost money; they had spent it.

BUILDING OUR SYSTEM

Our experience with Snapshot has been so positive that we've developed a new software system to automate this process. It's called TallyFin. By integrating with custodians and pulling real-time data, we provide clients with up-to-date Snapshots anytime they want to look at them.

This initiative further enhances our ability to control the narrative. Instead of reacting to client concerns after they receive confusing statements, we'll proactively provide them with clear, contextual information they can view online. We know when our clients get their custodial statements; we then send our Snapshot email for our clients to look at. That's controlling the narrative.

LEARNING FROM OTHER INDUSTRIES: THE ZAPPOS EXAMPLE

Controlling the narrative isn't unique to financial advising. Companies like Zappos have excelled by focusing on the customer experience. Zappos even gave up drop-shipping because they couldn't control the entire customer journey. If you haven't read their story, you should.

Similarly, we need to own the narrative with our clients. We can't let custodians dictate how our performance and value are perceived.

By providing tools like Snapshot and TallyFin, we take control of the narrative and enhance the client experience.

THE HUMOROUS SIDE OF SERIOUS BUSINESS

Well, financial advising isn't always laughs and giggles, but who says we can't inject a bit of humor?

When clients get fixated on their account value dropping due to their withdrawals, it's tempting to say, "Well, unless your money has discovered the secret to cloning itself, spending it will make the numbers go down." Of course, I opt for a more tactful approach, but a lighthearted comment can ease tension.

Or when discussing the complexities of cost basis and reinvested dividends, I might quip, "Think of your portfolio like a sourdough starter. You keep feeding it, it keeps growing, but unless you're a bread expert, it might look like a confusing blob."

EMBRACING THE ROLE OF EDUCATOR

At the end of the day, our role extends beyond managing assets; we're educators, guides, and sometimes therapists. By controlling the narrative, we help clients make informed decisions, reduce anxiety, and stay focused on their long-term goals.

We can't stop custodians from sending their standard statements, but we can provide context and clarity. The Snapshot is our way of saying, "Here's the full story, not just the headlines."

IMPLEMENTING THE SNAPSHOT IN CLIENT MEETINGS

Incorporating the Snapshot into client reviews has transformed our meetings. Instead of getting bogged down in explanations about cost basis discrepancies or market volatility, we focus on the comprehensive picture.

Clients are often amazed when they see the growth in their dividend income or realize how much they've withdrawn over the years. It cements our relationship and reinforces the value we bring.

ADDRESSING PERFORMANCE CONCERNS

The Snapshot also helps when clients question performance. If a client says, "I feel like my account hasn't grown much," we can point to the Snapshot and discuss the factors affecting their portfolio and where growth is most important, like their income.

Perhaps they've made significant withdrawals, or maybe the market has been volatile. The Snapshot provides the data needed to have an informed conversation.

STRENGTHENING STRATEGY AND EXECUTION

Interestingly, the process of creating Snapshots has also improved our internal processes. By regularly reviewing these key metrics, we gain insights into the effectiveness of our strategies.

We've noticed, for example, that portfolios requiring more frequent rebalancing due to client withdrawals tend to perform better. This has led us to reevaluate how we manage portfolios and consider more proactive rebalancing.

EMPOWERING CLIENTS

Ultimately, Snapshot empowers clients. It gives them a clear understanding of their financial situation, enabling them to make better decisions.

We always emphasize that they are the heroes of their financial journey. They've saved, invested, and trusted us to guide them. The Snapshot is a testament to their commitment and our partnership.

EMBRACE THE CHALLENGE

If you're an advisor struggling with similar issues, consider implementing a tool like the Snapshot. Start by gathering the four key metrics for each client and presenting them in a clear, concise format.

Remember, it's not about creating fancy charts or overwhelming clients with data. It's about telling their financial story in a way that makes sense to them.

Controlling the narrative isn't easy. It requires effort, attention to detail, and a commitment to putting the client's needs first. But the rewards are worth it.

You'll build stronger relationships, reduce misunderstandings, and provide a level of service that sets you apart from others in the industry.

BE THE HERO THEY NEED

Remember my medical misadventure from the start of this chapter? The doctors were so engrossed in their procedures and protocols that they forgot about me, the patient. Let's not make the same mistake with our clients.

By staying attuned to their needs, communicating effectively, and providing them with a narrative they can understand, we become more than just financial advisors. We become trusted partners in their life's journey.

Take control of the narrative. Your clients and your peace of mind will thank you.

CHAPTER 18

DON'T BE A LONE WOLF

Collaboration Elevates Every Advisor's Success

If you've been in the financial advising business long enough, you know we're a peculiar breed. We guard our client lists like they're the last slice of pizza at a party, and we often operate on islands—beautiful tropical islands with no Wi-Fi and absolutely zero collaboration.

Years ago, I was firmly settled on my island, happily sipping my coconut water, when I noticed a peculiar trend. Advisors started approaching me, eager to "look over my shoulder" to see how I was growing my practice. Now, let's be honest: when another advisor wants to shadow you, your first thought isn't "Oh joy, a new friend!" No, it's more along the lines of "What are you trying to steal from me?"

I had my guard up higher than a cat in a room full of rocking chairs. The younger you are in this business, the more open you are to sharing. Your book of business is wide open, and you're excited about the next best marketing concept. But the more established you become, the more you start building walls around your client base. You're just one bad marketing program or one ill-advised client remark away from a disaster.

So there I was, suspicious and somewhat amused by these advisors who wanted to peek behind the curtain. Then it hit me—if they wanted to look over my shoulder, perhaps I could look over theirs. I proposed a deal: "Come to my office, and let's invite a couple of other advisors. I'll share some of my strategies, but you have to share yours too." If they were going to "borrow" my ideas, I might as well "borrow" theirs. Fair trade, right?

THE BIRTH OF THE STUDY GROUP

Little did I know this was the humble beginning of something extraordinary—a catalyst for incredible growth for all of us. We didn't just exchange ideas; we sparked a movement. We called those meetups our study groups, where like-minded financial advisors would gather to share, learn, and yes, occasionally commiserate over the complexities of our profession.

Initially, we met once, thinking it would be a one-time gig. But then it became twice a year, then quarterly, and before we knew it, we were meeting so often we considered installing bunk beds in the office. The study groups became our way of getting out of ruts, especially during the ebbs and flows that are inevitable in this business. When times are good, they're great. But when times are tough, they're brutal. The camaraderie and shared wisdom of the group became our lifeline.

One of the first things we noticed was that this business can feel incredibly lonely. You're kind of on an island, doing your thing, and while you might know other advisors, they don't do things the same way you do. They might run the same seminars but approach them differently. We realized even though we're in the same industry, our experiences are unique, and that's where the power lies.

FROM ISOLATION TO INSPIRATION

I recall attending events hosted by FMOs (field marketing organizations) early in my career. You'd qualify for a trip or a conference, and suddenly you'd be rubbing shoulders with other advisors. For a brief moment, you'd feel connected. You'd exchange business cards, maybe even a few ideas, and then you'd return to your office fired up, ready to conquer the world. But that energy would fade, and soon enough, you'd find yourself back on your island.

Our study groups changed that dynamic entirely. We weren't just meeting occasionally to pat each other on the back. We were actively engaging with one another, sharing what was working and what wasn't. We required that every advisor bring ideas to the table. This wasn't a spectator sport; participation was mandatory.

One of our members mentioned that being part of the group was like having access to a Rolodex of advice. If he faced a situation he hadn't encountered before, there was a high likelihood that someone in the group had. It was like having a team of seasoned veterans at your disposal.

THE MOMENTUM EFFECT

Another advisor pointed out that the study group acted as a momentum pusher, not a momentum killer. In this business, momentum is everything. You have good months and bad months, but maintaining consistent growth can be challenging. Being part of a group of like-minded individuals who all want to see each other succeed creates a rising tide that lifts all boats.

We even had advisors who'd been in the business longer than some of us had been alive. Now, that's both impressive and a tad unsettling (and yes, I'm pointing at you, seasoned veterans). Their wealth of experience was invaluable. They could offer insights that only come from decades in the trenches.

Our clients began to notice the difference too. They appreciated that they weren't just getting one advisor's perspective but had an entire team supporting their financial future. If I was unavailable, they knew someone else equally capable could step in. It provided them with a sense of security and trust that's hard to build when you're flying solo.

One advisor mentioned, "You can go to our website and see the team. It's not just me on an island. I'm not just one person making decisions about your financial future in a vacuum. There's a whole organization surrounding me, supporting me."

SHARED SUCCESS STORIES

Perhaps one of the most inspiring moments was when an advisor who had been relatively stagnant suddenly caught fire. His production tripled in a year. Curious, I asked him what sparked this incredible growth.

"At the end of the last study group, I looked around the room and realized I didn't want to be the one sitting here next year without significant progress," he said. "The motivation I felt in that room was electric. I tapped into the community, sought help, and pushed myself harder than ever before."

His story wasn't unique. Many of us found that the collective energy and shared goals propelled us to new heights. We collaborated on cases, shared commissions, and even comanaged assets under management. It was like forming a superhero team, but instead of capes, we had calculators, and instead of superpowers, we had financial acumen.

INNOVATION THROUGH COLLABORATION

One of the unexpected benefits was how our collective ideas began to shape our practices. For instance, the Snapshot, which I've mentioned several times now and which gives clients a quick overview of their financial standing, came from an idea in a study group. Initially, I wasn't sold on the idea. It came from another advisor in the group who had been using it successfully.

I thought, "Nah, there's nothing there." But then I encountered a client situation where it would have been the perfect solution. I revisited the concept, and we integrated it into our practices. It evolved into something even more powerful—a tool that is revolutionizing the financial planning industry.

Similarly, our Simplicitree software underwent significant transformations thanks to the input from the group. What started as an Excel spreadsheet on a MacBook trying to calculate a rate of return morphed into a sophisticated platform that has become indispensable in our practice.

THE POWER OF NOT BEING ALONE

One advisor summed it up beautifully: "You're not on an island anymore. You're with a group of like-minded individuals who all want to do good for their clients. We all want to lift up everybody. The tide goes up; we all want to go up."

Another added, "The biggest thing I hate in my business is momentum killers. But this isn't one—this is a momentum pusher. You're surrounded by like-minded individuals, and every time you leave a study group, you walk away with at least one idea you can immediately put into action and improve how you run your business."

We even had some lighthearted moments. Early on, we learned not to challenge certain members to a game of pool or "double-tap" golf. Trust me, some of these folks could hustle a pool shark out of his fins. It's all fun and games until you realize you're buying the next round.

THE CLIENT'S PERSPECTIVE

Our collaborative approach didn't just benefit us. It also significantly enhanced our client relationships. Clients felt more secure knowing they had a team working on their behalf. If one advisor was unavailable, another could step in seamlessly. This collective expertise provided them with a richer, more comprehensive service.

An advisor mentioned, "Clients love that there's a whole organization surrounding me, supporting me. If you can't get me, if I'm sick, there's someone else who can step in and help out in that situation."

CONTINUOUS GROWTH AND DEVELOPMENT

The study groups also became a breeding ground for innovation. We developed new programs and strategies, many of which originated from casual conversations during our meetings. Ideas that we might have dismissed individually gained traction when the group saw their potential.

For example, the "shortfall" concept was something I initially came up with, but it was inspired by discussions within the group. The investment planning module we use wasn't my idea either. It was born out of collaborative brainstorming.

STEPPING OFF THE ISLAND

What's the takeaway here? In a profession that often feels isolating, the power of community is transformative. You don't have to join our study group—though the door is always open—but I can't stress enough the importance of finding or creating a community of your own. The collaboration, the shared wisdom, and yes, even the friendly competition, can propel your business in ways you can't achieve alone.

As financial advisors, we all have something to share and something to learn. The more open we are about "giving our business away," not just to our clients but to our peers, the more growth we can all experience. It's counterintuitive, I know. In a field where proprietary strategies and client lists are guarded closely, opening up can feel risky. But the rewards far outweigh the risks.

Think of it this way: Alone, we're a single note. Together, we create a symphony.

So, whether you decide to tap into an existing community or build your own, take that step. Reach out to other advisors, share your ideas, and be willing to learn from theirs. You might just find the island you've been on isn't so isolated after all.

And who knows? You might even pick up a few golf tips along the way. Just be careful whom you challenge to a game of pool.

Here are some key takeaways I want to share:

- **Don't Go It Alone:** The financial advising business doesn't have to be a solitary journey. Find a community to share ideas and challenges.
- **Be Open to Sharing:** By opening up your practice to others, you invite growth not just for yourself but for your peers as well.
- **Learn from Others:** Everyone has unique experiences and strategies. Tapping into this collective wisdom can provide solutions you hadn't considered.
- **Client Benefits:** A collaborative approach can enhance client trust and satisfaction, because they know they have a team working for their financial well-being.
- **Continuous Improvement:** Regular interaction with like-minded professionals keeps you motivated and helps you stay ahead of industry trends.

In the world of finance, collaboration isn't just a nice-to-have—it's a game changer. So step off your island and join the party. Just watch out for the guy with the uncanny pool skills.

PRACTICAL STEPS TO BUILDING YOUR COMMUNITY

1. **Start Small:** Invite a couple of advisors you respect to meet and share ideas. It doesn't have to be formal; the key is open dialogue.
2. **Set Expectations:** Ensure that everyone understands the value of mutual sharing. Each member should bring something to the table.
3. **Regular Meetings:** Consistency is crucial. Whether it's quarterly or monthly, set a schedule that keeps the momentum going.
4. **Diverse Perspectives:** Include advisors with varying levels of experience. The mix of fresh ideas and seasoned wisdom can be incredibly powerful.
5. **Leverage Technology:** Use online platforms for virtual meetings if distance is an issue. The goal is connection, not proximity.
6. **Be Open to Change:** Allow the group to evolve. What starts as a simple idea exchange can grow into something much more impactful.

The secret sauce isn't a proprietary strategy or groundbreaking software—it's the community. It's the collective effort of individuals willing to share, learn, and grow together. In an industry that's ever changing and often unpredictable, having a support system can make all the difference.

So go ahead; take the plunge. You might just find the journey is a lot more enjoyable—and profitable—when you have companions along the way.

CHAPTER 19

MARSHMALLOWS

Skip the Quick Fix and Wait for the Bigger Reward

I still remember the first time I heard about the "Marshmallow Test."[5] I was at a conference, half listening to a keynote speaker who launched into this story about little kids, a single marshmallow, and a monumental test of willpower. At first, I figured, "Okay, it's just some cute psychology anecdote." But as the speaker went on, I found myself leaning forward in my seat. I realized this wasn't just about kids and candy. It was a vivid illustration of how we humans handle (or struggle with) delayed gratification. By the end of it, I couldn't help thinking, "This story could apply so perfectly to us financial advisors." Because, let's be honest, we have our version of that marshmallow every day.

Here's the story as it was shared with me:

Imagine a room filled with a group of four-year-old boys and girls sitting around a table. There's a plate set in front of each child, and on each plate is a single marshmallow. The room is quiet except for

---

5   Walter Mischel et al., "Cognitive and Attentional Mechanisms in Delay of Gratification," *Journal of Personality and Social Psychology* 21, no. 2 (1972): 204–18. https://doi.org/10.1037/h0032198.

the occasional rustle of clothing and the soft sounds of suppressed giggles. A researcher kneels to eye level with each child and delivers the ultimate test of wills:

"You can eat your marshmallow now," the researcher says, "but if you wait until I return, you'll get a second one."

The door closes. The countdown begins.

Some children stare intently at their marshmallow as if trying to unlock its secrets through sheer force of will. Others poke, prod, or even sniff their marshmallow, their faces contorted in concentration.

One particularly imaginative boy turns around in his chair, refusing to even look at the sugary temptation. A girl hums a tune, swinging her legs and clapping her hands in a desperate attempt to distract herself.

Minutes feel like hours in marshmallow time.

Finally, one brave soul leans in, eyes darting to the door, and gives the marshmallow a quick lick—as if calories don't count if it's just a taste. Another taps his foot impatiently, muttering under his breath, "Come on, come on, come on…" A few can't take the suspense any longer and gobble up the marshmallow, cheeks puffed out like squirrels storing nuts for winter.

When the researcher finally returns, some children beam with pride, their marshmallows untouched, while others look sheepish, a few sticky remnants betraying their moment of weakness.

This is the famous Marshmallow Test, a psychological experiment designed by Walter Mischel in the 1960s to study delayed gratification. The children's struggles are both hilarious and deeply human, revealing the inner battle between immediate desire and long-term reward.

When I first heard this story, I couldn't shake off how unbelievably relevant it felt to financial advising. We guide clients who face their versions of "marshmallows" every day—whether it's chasing a quick market win, falling for the newest shiny marketing tactic, or bailing out too soon on a thoughtful investment plan. As advisors, we're also tested: do we hold out for that second marshmallow (a deeper client relationship, a more sustainable practice model), or do we grab the quick fix right away?

This is what makes this story so important: it captures, in the simplest possible way, the tension between short-term impulses and long-term success. I'll never forget hearing it and instantly thinking, "This is for financial advisors. This is exactly what we do. If we can help clients hold out for the second marshmallow, we all come out ahead."

WHY THE MARSHMALLOW MATTERS

The Marshmallow Test is a window into how we handle temptation, delay gratification, and make decisions that affect our future selves. Long-term studies have shown that the children who managed to wait for the second marshmallow tended to have better life outcomes. They scored higher on the SAT, had lower levels of substance abuse, managed stress more effectively, and even had lower body mass indices.

According to Mischel's follow-up research, about two-thirds of the children couldn't resist the marshmallow. That's a lot of sticky fingers! But the one-third who waited showcased a trait that's crucial for success in virtually every field: patience.

THE STATS ON WAITING

Let's dig into some numbers:

- **Academic Performance:** Children who delayed gratification scored an average of 210 points higher on the SAT.
- **Health Outcomes:** They had a 30 percent lower risk of obesity by adulthood.
- **Financial Stability:** Adults who practiced delayed gratification

had higher credit scores and were less likely to experience financial hardships.[6]

These stats underscore a fundamental truth: patience isn't just a virtue; it's a predictor of success.

Why is it so hard to wait? For one, humans are hardwired for immediate rewards. Our ancestors needed to prioritize immediate needs—like eating and shelter—to survive. In today's world, this wiring doesn't always serve us well. We live in an era of instant gratification: instant messaging, same-day delivery, and streaming services that eliminate the wait between episodes.

Patience requires effort. It demands we override our natural impulses, and that's no small feat. The prefrontal cortex—the part of the brain responsible for self-control—isn't fully developed until our mid-twenties. Even then, it competes with the limbic system, which is all about reward and pleasure.

LESSONS IN PATIENCE

What can we learn from a bunch of kids wrestling with marshmallow-induced angst?

1. **Distraction Helps:** Many kids who succeeded did so by distracting themselves—singing songs, covering their eyes, or turning away. In our lives, redirecting our focus can help us resist temptations.
2. **Visualization Matters:** Imagining the future reward as vividly as possible can make waiting easier. Envisioning that second marshmallow—or the benefits of a well-thought-out financial plan—can bolster patience.

---

6   Mischel's follow-up studies found higher SAT scores and better life outcomes for kids who delayed gratification. See Walter Mischel, *The Marshmallow Test: Mastering Self-Control* (Little, Brown and Company, 2014).

3. **Environment Counts:** Creating an environment with fewer temptations makes it easier to wait. Just as removing the marshmallow from sight helped some kids, minimizing immediate distractions can keep us on track toward long-term goals.

THE FINANCIAL ADVISOR'S MARSHMALLOW

Financial advisors often find themselves in a high-stakes version of the Marshmallow Test. The "marshmallows" in our industry are the tempting shortcuts that promise immediate rewards but jeopardize long-term success.

Consider aggressive email marketing tactics. This is when an advisor blasts out mass emails in hopes of attracting new prospects. The allure is strong—quick responses, immediate interest, and the thrill of adding new clients overnight. It's like grabbing that marshmallow the moment the researcher leaves the room. But this approach often leaves a sour aftertaste, damaging reputations and eroding trust when promises fall short. This is a single marshmallow.

Then there are the "always dependable" internet leads. Financial advisors purchase thousands of internet leads every day. It's tempting to think that more leads equals more clients. This marshmallow promises a shortcut to building a client base without the painstaking process of networking and relationship building. But chasing these cold leads can lead to frustration, lost time, and wasted resources, much like the kids who couldn't resist and ended up with only one marshmallow instead of two.

Lastly, we have the shiny objects—the next trendy marketing tactic that's gaining traction. Maybe it's a new social media platform where advisors are suddenly flocking or a flashy software tool that promises to revolutionize client acquisition with minimal effort. The temptation here is to jump on the bandwagon, to grab that marshmallow while it's hot, hoping for instant results without fully understanding how it fits into a long-term strategy.

These marshmallows are hard to resist. The temptation to secure immediate results can be overwhelming, especially when competitors seem to race ahead, much like children sneaking glances at their peers to see who's indulging.

Remember my wild ride on Thunderbolt from the beginning of this book? Just as I wasn't prepared to handle a racehorse, advisors who rush into these quick fixes without building a solid foundation may find themselves clinging for dear life—or worse, losing control of their practice entirely.

The desire to move fast—to gobble up that first marshmallow— can lead to short-term gains but long-term pains. Clients today are savvy; they can sense when an advisor is more interested in quick commissions than in building lasting relationships. They, too, are looking for that second marshmallow—the assurance that their advisor is committed to their long-term financial well-being.

By resisting these tempting marshmallows and focusing instead on cultivating genuine relationships, honing your expertise, and developing a personalized approach, you position yourself for enduring success. Just like the children who waited patiently and reaped greater rewards, advisors who embrace patience and discipline will find the benefits far outweigh the allure of immediate gratification.

BUILDING YOUR OWN STABLE

Instead of chasing after someone else's process or sprinting toward immediate gratification, consider the value of building your stable on a strong foundation—a foundation supported by three unbreakable pillars: client experience, planning, and investment strategy.

Just as a stable needs a solid base to house powerful horses, your financial practice requires these three elements working in harmony. There's a verse in the Bible that says, "A cord of three strands is not quickly broken" (Ecclesiastes 4:12).

While the context speaks to the strength of unity, the principle applies here: when client experience, planning, and investment strategy are tightly woven together, they form a resilient foundation for your practice. Remove one, and the entire structure weakens. Let's delve into each of these crucial components.

CLIENT EXPERIENCE

Investing in your clients goes beyond standard service. It's about creating meaningful experiences that build trust and loyalty.

- **Understand Their Needs:** Take the time to genuinely listen to your clients. What are their fears? What are their dreams? By understanding their unique circumstances, you can tailor your services to meet their specific needs.
- **Personalized Interactions:** One size doesn't fit all. Customize your communication and engagement strategies for each client. This could mean remembering important milestones, sending personalized notes, or adapting your meetings to their preferred style.
- **Build Lasting Relationships:** Trust isn't built overnight. Consistently demonstrate reliability and integrity in all your interactions. When clients feel valued and understood, they're more likely to stay with you for the long haul.

PLANNING

A well-thought-out plan is the blueprint for success, both for your clients and your practice. We are biased here with Simplicitree and believe there isn't a better planning solution on the market that can match its simplicity, interaction, and client ownership. If you don't believe me, take it out for a spin and see for yourself.

- **Client Shortfall:** The first place you need to start planning is to know and understand a client's shortfall, as it's the difference between where they are and where they want to be. It's the income gap that keeps them up at night.
- **Client Ownership:** When a client takes ownership of their income plan, you get to rest at night and can have peace of mind that when the next big market correction occurs, you are not going to lose them as a client. Ownership changes everything.
- **Adaptability:** Life is full of unexpected changes. Regularly review and adjust plans to reflect new circumstances, ensuring that strategies remain aligned with your clients' evolving needs.

INVESTMENT STRATEGY

Your investment strategy is the engine that drives a client's most important need—their retirement income. Growth matters, but nothing is more important than income.

- **Dividend Growth:** Develop investment portfolios that not only aim for capital appreciation but also provide a steady income stream through dividends. This dual approach offers clients the potential for growth while supplying regular income, catering to both their short-term needs and long-term goals.
- **Needs-Based Risk Management:** Instead of focusing solely on a client's comfort level with risk, assess the level of risk necessary to achieve their specific income requirements and financial goals. This "needs-based" approach ensures the investment strategy is purposefully designed to meet their objectives without exposing them to unnecessary risk.

- **Empowering Through Education:** Equip your clients with the knowledge they need to understand various investment strategies. By clearly explaining which approaches are effective and which are not, you empower them to make informed decisions and take ownership of their financial future.

By integrating these components—Dividend Growth, Needs-Based Risk Management, and Empowering Through Education—you enhance the effectiveness of your investment strategy. This comprehensive approach not only aims for optimal financial performance but also builds deeper trust and engagement with your clients.

When your clients see that their investment strategy provides steady income, aligns with their specific needs, and is something they actively understand and participate in, they are more likely to remain committed and confident in their financial journey with you.

EMBRACE PATIENCE AND BUILD FOR THE LONG TERM

Building such a strong foundation isn't a rapid process; it requires patience, dedication, and a focus on long-term success over short-term wins. Just as the children who waited in the Marshmallow Test received a greater reward, advisors who invest time and effort into these core areas will cultivate practices that are both sustainable and profitable.

Instead of being tempted by quick fixes or the allure of immediate gratification, focus on constructing your own stable, one that can house many horses and stand the test of time. By committing to excellence in client experience, meticulous planning, and sound investment strategy, you're not just holding on for the ride; you're confidently leading the charge.

Remember, the strength of your practice lies in the unity of these three elements. Together, they form an unbreakable foundation that can withstand market volatility, competitive pressures, and the evolving needs of your clients.

So let's build that strong stable. Invest in your clients, craft thoughtful plans, and develop investment strategies that drive success. When you do, you'll discover you're not only achieving your professional goals but also making a lasting difference in the lives of those you serve.

RIDE OFF INTO THE SUNSET

Reflecting on that youthful version of me, clutching the reins of a horse I had no business riding, I understand that I wanted the thrill, the bragging rights, and maybe a nod of approval from my high school crush. But I skipped the essential steps—learning to ride, understanding the horse, and respecting the process.

Similarly, those kids in the Marshmallow Test who couldn't wait represent the part of us that's tempted to take shortcuts. But shortcuts often lead to dead ends—or at least to sticky situations that could have been avoided.

The next time you're tempted to grab that marshmallow or mount that untamed horse, pause for a moment. Consider the power of patience and the value of the journey. Remember, the goal isn't just to reach the destination but to arrive equipped, prepared, and ready to lead.

If you take the time to build your stable and nurture your horses, you'll never want to ride someone else's horse again. Who knows? Along the way, you might find the ride itself is the most rewarding part of all.

DO YOU TRUST ME?

Find Limitless Success by Giving Freely

Years ago, I stood at the crossroads of my career, not realizing that a profound lesson was about to reshape not only my business but my entire approach to life.

As a typical financial advisor, I was entrenched in the daily grind of growing my business, conducting seminars, purchasing leads online, and leveraging my existing clients for referrals. While the foundational principles I've shared throughout this book were present, I was far from the understanding and success I experience today.

At that time, I was a member of C12, a Christian business owners' group that brings together men and women from diverse industries—plumbers, electricians, software developers, home builders, and yes, financial advisors like me. The purpose was simple yet profound: to ground our businesses in faith, hold each other accountable, and learn from one another despite the differences in our industries.

One day, Tony, the leader of our C12 group, approached me with a request. "I have another member who wants to join our group," he said. "You know who he is, and I'd like your blessing to allow him in."

My heart sank. The individual in question was not just any financial advisor; he was a titan in our industry. The owner of a much larger practice, he managed many billions in assets and led a team of 180 advisors. If I were part of his firm, I would have been his top advisor—a fact that hadn't escaped his notice. He often sought my opinions during his occasional visits, curious about my strategies and successes.

I felt a knot tighten in my stomach. Letting him into our intimate group felt like inviting a lion into a lamb's den. I consulted with my peers, and unanimously, they advised against it.

"You'll be too afraid to share openly," they warned. "He could take your ideas and overshadow you."

Their concerns echoed my fears. Up to that point, my philosophy had been clear: give enough to your clients to earn their trust and business, but not so much that they no longer need you. Knowledge was power, and power was best kept close to the vest.

That night, as I wrestled with my decision, I awoke in a cold sweat. A voice—gentle yet unmistakable—stirred within me. "Do you trust me?" it asked.

I knew it was God speaking to my heart. "Of course I trust you," I replied silently.

"Then I not only want you to allow this advisor into your group," He continued, "but I want you to sit down with him and share everything about your business—all your secrets, your strategies, your innermost thoughts."

I was stunned. "Everything?" I questioned. "You want me to bare my soul to a competitor who could easily crush me?"

"Yes," He affirmed. "Do you trust me?"

The following day, I met with Tony. "Against all conventional wisdom, I feel led to welcome this other advisor into our group," I told him. "God is guiding my decision."

Soon after, I invited the advisor to lunch. Over the meal, I extended an offer that felt both liberating and terrifying. "I'd like to invite you to my office," I said. "I want to share everything about my business with you."

To my surprise, he accepted eagerly.

In my office, I laid it all out—the way we managed money, our marketing strategies, the software we were developing, our future plans. I held nothing back. I expected to feel vulnerable, but instead, a sense of peace washed over me.

Up to that point, my business had been growing steadily at about 40 percent annually—a respectable rate by any measure. But after that meeting, something extraordinary happened. The following year, our growth nearly doubled, and it continued to do so year after year.

I began to understand a profound truth: when you give freely, blessings return to you manifold. It's a biblical principle—"Give, and it will be given to you" (Luke 6:38). By opening my hands and releasing what I had clutched so tightly, I made room to receive more than I could have imagined.

This shift didn't just affect my business; it permeated every aspect of my life. I no longer felt the need to guard my knowledge or hold back from my clients. Transparency became my new currency. When clients asked questions, I gave them complete answers. If I didn't know something, I admitted it and committed to finding the answer. I took full ownership of my actions and decisions, embracing accountability like never before.

One tangible example of this transformation was how I began managing assets. Previously, I outsourced asset management to others, which allowed me to deflect responsibility when things didn't go well. "It's the manager's fault," I would say. But now I manage assets personally. When performance dips, I don't dodge accountability. I have honest conversations with my clients about market conditions and reaffirm my commitment to our long-term strategy.

Another example is in client education. I used to believe that if

I taught clients too much, they wouldn't need me anymore. But the more I educated them, the more they valued our relationship. They appreciated the transparency and referred others who were seeking the same level of openness.

The advisors I've mentored who have adopted this philosophy have seen similar results. Those who fully own their practices—who internalize their strategies, embrace accountability, and share openly—experience significantly greater success than those who merely follow the crowd.

As we conclude this journey together, I want to leave you with this: ownership and generosity are catalysts for exponential growth. When you take full responsibility for every aspect of your business—your strategies, your decisions, your interactions—you empower yourself to operate at your highest potential. And when you couple that ownership with a willingness to give freely of your knowledge and resources, you unlock a cycle of blessings that propels you forward.

Don't hold back. Share your wisdom, your insights, your very best with others—even your competitors. Trust that in giving, you are planting seeds that will yield a harvest beyond your wildest dreams.

Remember, this isn't just about business growth; it's about personal transformation. It's about stepping into a life marked by abundance, integrity, and profound fulfillment.

As you close this book and step back into the world, I challenge you to embrace the power of giving it all away. Let go of the fear that sharing diminishes you. Instead, recognize that generosity multiplies your impact.

Own your journey. Be transparent with your clients, your colleagues, and yourself. When challenges come up, face them head-on with integrity and accountability. When successes come, share them as a testament to the principles you've adopted.

Your potential is limitless when you operate from a place of trust, openness, and wholehearted commitment. So go forward and build not just a successful business, but a legacy that inspires others to do the same.

You have everything you need within you. Give freely, own fully, and watch as your life transforms in ways you never thought possible.

ACKNOWLEDGMENTS

To every advisor who has ever rolled their eyes at a marketing pitch, sat through a seminar wondering if there was a better way, or tried to cram "deep client experience" into a forty-seven-minute Zoom call—this book is for you.

To the advisors who showed up at one of our study groups ready to learn, question, and challenge my thinking—thank you. You've pushed me to grow, kept me humble, and made this profession a lot less lonely.

To the clients who trusted me with their stories, their spreadsheets, and their fears about the future—you've been the greatest teachers I never knew I needed. You helped me see that this job isn't about transactions—it's about transformation.

To the team at Insight Folios and Uplift Technologies—you've turned wild ideas, half-finished metaphors, and "what if we built this" moments into real tools that advisors and clients now rely on every day. You bring vision to life with humility, brilliance, and far too many sticky notes. I'm grateful for each of you.

To Kevin, Kyle, Niki, Ryan, and every advisor who's opened up their practice so we could all build something bigger than ourselves—your honesty, your encouragement, and your willingness to "give it all away" have shaped more than this book. You've shaped a movement.

To everyone at Scribe Media—thank you for helping me shape this book into something I can truly be proud of. You took a mountain of content and helped me carve out the heart of it with care, creativity, and expertise. This would not be the same book without you. I don't need to name you all by name, but please know your fingerprints are on every page—and I'm deeply grateful.

To Daniel, a good friend and an even better idea machine—thank you for letting me toss a million and one ideas your way and for always tossing something better right back. You make life richer and work more fun, and this book is far better than it would have been without you.

To my wife, Stephanie—thank you for letting me test stories, metaphors, and meeting frameworks over dinner. You've endured more advisor analogies than anyone ever should, and you still laugh at the good ones (and kindly ignore the bad ones).

To Evan, Shane, and Reid—thanks for letting me be your coach, your dad, and your practice client. You remind me that the best work we'll ever do has nothing to do with charts, compound interest, or rebalancing models—and everything to do with showing up.

And finally, to the One who makes all things new—thank You for reminding me that I don't need to be the hero of anyone's story. I just need to serve the people God places in front of me. Everything I've built, taught, and written flows from that truth.

This book may have my name on the cover, but it carries the fingerprints of so many. Thank you for letting me learn from you, write about you, and build alongside you.

ABOUT THE AUTHOR

PAUL DURSO is a financial advisor, entrepreneur, and creator of tools like Simplicitree, TallyFin, and Unifi CRM—solutions that turn financial planning from a passive experience into a deeply personal journey.

He's the founder of Insight Folios and Uplift Technologies, and the author of *Moneywork: Fuel Your Freedom with Dividend Income*. He's been featured on CBS, FOX, NBC, and a few client dinner napkins when inspiration struck faster than the check could arrive.

Paul is best known for teaching advisors how to grow their business without chasing cold leads, confusing clients, or burning themselves out. His approach? Co-planning. Education first. And a whole lot of client experience built on clarity, not complexity.

A Certified Estate Planner, Certified Wealth Strategist, and Certified Retirement Planner (yes, he collects credentials like some people collect vinyl), Paul still considers his most important titles to be Husband, Dad, and Follower of Jesus.

When he's not coaching advisors, writing books, or hosting podcasts, you'll find him taking a nap, trying to fix his golf swing, or chasing his three turbo-charged sons: Evan, Shane, and Reid. He lives in Charlotte, North Carolina, with his wife, Stephanie, who reminds him daily that the best plans involve flip-flops, family, and dinner around the table.